I0616076

About

BIBLICAL
CHURCH
Governance

Register This New Book

Benefits of Registering*

- ✓ FREE **replacements** of lost or damaged books
- ✓ FREE **audiobook** – *Pilgrim's Progress,* audiobook edition
- ✓ FREE information about new titles and other **freebies**

www.anekopress.com/new-book-registration

*See our website for requirements and limitations.

The Church is Jesus' bride. Those who are called to lead this beautiful bride must do so with humility, grace, and diligence. Stephen Gammon's book is an excellent guide to help us see the ways to accomplish this sacred responsibility. I heartily recommend Steve's book. He has honorably lived out what he writes.

Rev. Dr. Marc S. Gauthier
Conference Minister, Conservative Congregational Christian Conference (CCCC)

Rev. Dr. Stephen Gammon's book lives up to its title. He clearly presents biblical principles for local churches in a warm and concise manner, supported by decades of pastoral, denominational, and international ministry experience. I was privileged to witness some of this excellent material taught by Stephen to pastors, elders, and deacons in Nepal, as these timeless biblical principles apply to all local churches, internationally and cross-culturally. This is a well-organized and approachable book that encourages and enables readers who seek to know and apply God's clear standards for churches. I am delighted to commend it to local church leaders and all members who are interested in the health of their churches.

Rev. Alan Best
Padstow Chinese Congregational Church, NSW, Australia, and Ambassador, World Evangelical Congregational Fellowship (WECF)

Dr. Gammon's trustworthy distillation of ministry in the local church is clearly presented through the biblical concepts of headship, leadership, and membership – the God-given design for the Body of Christ, regardless of denominational affiliation – a must-read and reread for those in vestry ministry. Formidable but straightforward, this volume facilitates the natural renewing of the mind and commitment to Christ as Head, to the gravity of leadership in the light of the empowerment of membership through the Holy Spirit.

Fr. Robert J. Geoffrey
Church of the Apostles (Anglican), Coventry, RI, USA

About
BIBLICAL
CHURCH
Governance

Biblical Principles
for *Being* and *Leading*
Local Churches

Stephen A. Gammon

ANEKO
PRESS

www.walkingwithgodforlife.com

About Biblical Church Governance

© 2025 by Stephen A. Gammon

All rights reserved. Published 2025.

Please do not reproduce, store in a retrieval system, or transmit in any form or by any means – electronic, mechanical, photocopying, recording, or otherwise, without written permission from the publisher.

Scripture quotations are taken from the Holy Bible, New Living Translation, copyright ©1996, 2004, 2015 by Tyndale House Foundation. Used by permission of Tyndale House Publishers, Carol Stream, Illinois 60188. All rights reserved.

Cover Designer: Jonathan Lewis

Editors: Paul Miller

Aneko Press

www.anekopress.com

Aneko Press, Life Sentence Publishing, and our logos are trademarks of

Life Sentence Publishing, Inc.
203 E. Birch Street
P.O. Box 652
Abbotsford, WI 54405

RELIGION / Christian Church / Administration

Paperback ISBN: 979-8-88936-511-2

eBook ISBN: 979-8-88936-512-9

10 9 8 7 6 5 4 3 2 1

Available where books are sold

Contents

Foreword ix

Preface xiii

Introduction xxi

Ch. 1: What the Church Truly Is...1

Ch. 2: Contrived Images of What the Church Is Not..23

Ch. 3: Primary Forms of Historic Church Governance....................................41

Ch. 4: Levels of Authority and Responsibility in Biblical Local Churches....53

Ch. 5: Essential Faith Convictions of Historic Biblical Governance..............77

Ch. 6: Cautions of Carefulness in Biblical Local Church Governance 113

An Addendum 151

Other Titles by Stephen A. Gammon.. 171

Foreword

Pastors and church leaders have been given a great trust. They have been assigned by God to lead the Church of Christ for the advancement of the Kingdom of God in this world. Jesus said, *I will build my church* (Matthew 16:18). It is His church. Yet in God's divine plan, He has entrusted ordinary people like us to lead and guide the Church until Jesus returns in glory.

Paul describes the vastness of God's grace, love, and power in Ephesians 3. He concludes this teaching by saying,

> *Now to him who is able to do immeasurably more than*
> *all we ask or imagine, according to his power that is at*
> *work within us, to him be glory in the church and in Christ*
> *Jesus throughout all generations, for ever and ever! Amen.*
> (Ephesians 3:20-21)

We must prayerfully contemplate these words so we can fully grasp this teaching. God is at work to do mighty, life-changing things that are beyond comprehension. He has chosen to do this through the Church. *To him be glory in the church and in Christ Jesus.* The Church reflects the glory of God as we carry out the glorious work of Christ. This work must not be taken lightly.

Dr. Stephen Gammon wrote this book to help us more fully understand the immense privilege of local church leadership. Steve is a third-generation pastor with five decades of pastoral-ministry experience. He is uniquely qualified to address church ministry, having faithfully served as a local church pastor and a denominational leader.

Dr. Gammon deeply explores and explains the nature of the Church of Jesus Christ. It is vital for pastors and local church leaders to fully grasp the role that the church is called to play in God's plan of salvation. The Church is more than a religious institution with a Jesus nameplate. It is integrally connected to Jesus Christ and to His work. It is a glorious representation of the Gospel for all generations.

This book provides great insights into ways that local churches are set apart from all human institutions. Dr. Gammon reminds us that a local church is not a building or a series of services and activities. It is also not a club for people assembled for mutual edification. Local churches are people gathered together under the lordship of Jesus Christ to continue His work, bringing the message of the gospel to a sinful and broken world.

Dr. Gammon also gets into the nitty-gritty of what it means to be a church leader and a member of a local church. This biblical teaching is important because it is where the rubber meets the road in the ways that a local church functions. He makes it clear that regardless of the polity of a local church, every pastor, leader, and member is accountable to God for the way that they exercise their role in the church. The Bible provides practical guidelines that must be followed for a local church to have fruitful ministry. These guidelines are all centered on Jesus Christ and His mission.

I found the personal reflection statements and the church leader's discussion questions to be especially helpful, as they help the reader take a moment to pause and pray about all that he or she has just read. They also open the door to listen to other people who share the work of the ministry. These are true "body building" tools that help this teaching come alive.

I was encouraged by reading this book, being excited about ways that pastors and local church leaders can effectively contribute to kingdom-building ministry in and through the local church. As I finished reading this book, I was prompted to spend time praying for the church.

Thank you, Lord, for the Church, which is Your instrument to bring the gospel to this world and in this generation. Strengthen each pastor and local church leader as they humbly serve You in their work. Help them to serve in ways that are in line with scriptural teaching and that reflect Your glory. Build Your Church, O Lord Jesus, and use it to power-fully do Your work in this generation. Amen.

– Rev. Dr. Ronald Hamilton
President of World Evangelical Congregational Fellowship
and former Conference Minister of CCCC USA

Preface

I t is with profound gratitude and praise to God for the Church of Jesus Christ that I was moved to write this book. The Church has been a major part of my life since early childhood. I was raised in a home where Jesus Christ was acknowledged and worshipped. My parents, Glendon and Marjorie Gammon, were dedicated to their faith and to the Church. My dad, who served as a pastor, and my mom, who was the daughter of a pastor, shared the same commitment to Jesus Christ and to His Church. Their dedication and service very deeply influenced me spiritually, perhaps akin to how many physical traits are passed down genetically.

I know well that I neither earned nor chose to be born into this Christian home or to be raised in the Church of Jesus. I did nothing to merit such love and grace, nor can any of us. Because we cannot earn or deserve God's favor, we must run from any temptations of spiritual pride.

God saved you by His grace when you believed. And you can't take credit for this; it is a gift from God. Salvation is not a reward for the good things we have done, so none of us can boast about it (Ephesians 2:8-9). We therefore rejoice in God's grace. All who have received God's free gift of salvation are in the Lord's Church, and we share this grace in common. God has given to us a priceless gift we never could have earned. We've received it entirely because of the love and grace of God, and through our genuine response of faith and love.

Jesus taught something that has been powerfully compelling for me, and it is for all who have received the grace of His salvation by faith. He said, *When someone has been given much, much will be required in return* (Luke 12:48). Does this speak to you as it speaks to me? All of us who know, believe, love, and follow Jesus Christ owe Him everything! To make this personal, can we all say to Jesus now, "Yes, Lord. I know it is true. I do owe You everything!"?

I am not alluding to a works-based religion of obligation, as though we are now compelled to work long and hard to pay off the debt that we owe Jesus. I am referring instead to a deeper, more satisfying, and lasting incentive: a motivation of love. We want to love, and we feel compelled to love the one who we know has loved us more than we have deserved or fully imagined or could ever aptly describe.

I first began to believe and understand God's great grace and love for me when I was a little boy. Such childlike faith brought me at about age five to get on my knees, ask Jesus to come into my heart, forgive me of my sins, and be my Savior. I knew then that Jesus loved me – and I loved Jesus. I still do.

The Lord Jesus knew that for me and you and all of God's children it would be a lifelong battle to hold on in faith to the transforming truth that we are deeply loved by God. To be motivated by God's love in life and ministry, we must truly believe that He loves us. When we know that we have sinned, the devil tempts us with a lie that God no longer deeply loves us, or even likes us, because we have sinned again.

Thankfully, God has given us many Scripture passages to dispel the lie and to reassure us of God's enduring love. But somewhat like taking medicine, it is only helpful if we take what God has prescribed for us. I am so blessed to have a God who has been throughout my life an ever-present, great physician who knows me well and always prescribes what I need to live, serve, and love according to His will.

Even today as I write this, I have a fresh example. Last night when I went to bed, I was wrestling again with my sinfulness, feeling unworthy to write a book like this, for I keep falling short of God's will for me. So I prayed, giving my struggle to the Lord. This morning I awoke with this medicine on my mind:

> *But God showed His great love for us by sending Christ to die for us while we were still sinners. And since we have been made right in God's sight by the blood of Christ, He will certainly save us from God's condemnation. For since our*

*friendship with God was restored by the death of his Son
while we were still his enemies, we will certainly be saved
through the life of his Son. So now we can rejoice in our
wonderful new relationship with God because our Lord Jesus
Christ has made us friends of God.* (Romans 5:8-11)

Amen! It is surely not because I have earned or deserved God's mercy
that I devoted my life to serving Jesus Christ and His Church. Rather, it
is because of God's great love for me, because I know what God's grace
is, and because I have received His grace through faith in Jesus. While we
were yet sinners (and even though I still sin), Christ died for me and for
you, thus making us worthy of His salvation (because of Christ). So we are
living now and forever in a relationship with God, even as friends of God.

I love Jesus, who has loved me so. It has been my lifelong desire to
follow Him all my days, to go wherever He sends me, to say whatever
He gives me to say, to serve however He leads me to serve, and to do
whatever He calls me to do. This has been the desire of my heart since
I was nineteen years old, when I heard my Lord's clear call to follow
and serve Him all of my days.

Everyone who has heard Jesus call them to *Come, follow me*
(Matthew 4:19), and has accepted His invitation, has a personal story
to tell of God's grace. Some of us came to know Jesus as little children.
Others came as teenagers or young adults, some came in midlife, others
in later life, and some near the end of their mortal life. In His parable of
vineyard workers, as told in Matthew 20:1-16, Jesus emphasized the grace
of God in calling people in various stages of life to come and follow Him.

But whenever God's grace reaches us, everyone who responds in
faith to His amazing offer of everlasting life has a story to tell. All who
choose in faith to follow Him have been given a testimony that needs
to be told. Again, as Jesus has taught us, *When someone has been given
much, much will be required in return* (Luke 12:48).

So here are some questions for each of us: How has God blessed
you? What has He given you? I know I was given much, and by God's
grace and in God's time, I heard His call for me to come follow Him
now, wherever He would lead me.

Having been born into a Christian home, I was very blessed to be raised in local churches. As a child and into my teen years, I whole-heartedly believed in Jesus, and I knew that the Bible was true. But as I entered my young adult years, it had not yet dawned on me that the one in whom I believed would have a plan for my life, or that He would surely lead me in His plan if I would only seek, listen, and follow.

This revelation came to me exactly fifty years ago from the day I am typing this page. That life-changing evening I was in the sanctuary of the Baptist church in Fair Haven, Vermont, cleaning the building in prepa-ration for worship services to be held the next day. Suddenly I became powerfully aware that I was in the presence of a holy God. I could not remain standing. I fell down, prostrate before the Lord, unable to move.

Then I heard my Lord ask me a question. If it was audible or in the Spirit, I do not know, but I heard the Lord clearly say, "Stephen Gammon, who will be Lord of your life – you or Me?"

In that holy moment, I could give just one reply: "You, Jesus! You are Lord of all! Be Lord of all in my life!" This was God's grace to me, and when I rose from that floor I was changed. I was filled with prayerful resolve to follow my Lord Jesus wherever and however He would lead me through all of life.

A few weeks after that life-changing encounter, God began making His leading clear for me. I was then a student at the University of Vermont, enrolled in classes for a pre-med or pre-dentistry program. That semester I had also gathered a group of college friends with whom I was studying and leading a weekly Bible study. After our study and prayer time one week, one of them said, "Steve, there is something we want to say to you."

"Sure. What is it?" I asked.

"We have discussed this, and we all agree that what you are doing with us is what God would have you do with your life."

When I heard those words, God the Holy Spirit immediately con-firmed that they were right. I determined then and there that I would obey. I knew Jesus was calling me to invest my life and energies in His Church, making and developing disciples of Jesus Christ. Soon after this, I transferred to Barrington College and majored in biblical stud-ies. There I met, fell in love with, and married Helen.

After finishing college, we moved to Minnesota where I studied at Bethel Theological Seminary, graduating three years later with a Master of Divinity degree. At the age of twenty-five, in Pawtucket, Rhode Island, I began my first assignment as a local church pastor. Although I was young, I had spent my life thus far in the Lord's Church, having been prepared by the Lord Jesus for this ministry.

I recall the deep humility I felt regarding the Lord's call upon my life, and my readiness to lead His church. It was on the day of my vicinage council, about six months after I had begun my duties as a local church pastor. In the tradition of Congregationalism, pastors and church leaders from nearby congregations had gathered that day at the invitation of the church I was serving. This council was called to consider and advise the local church regarding whether or not it was right for them to proceed with setting me apart for pastoral ordination. Representatives of about twenty nearby congregations came that day.

In advance of the council, I prepared and distributed a detailed paper telling my story of faith in the Lord Jesus. In it I described my sense of call to pastoral ministry, and I outlined my convictions about the major doctrines of the Christian faith, with biblical references supporting every statement I made.

The council questioned me that day about all I had written and said. They listened to my heart and testimony in order to prayerfully discern my spiritual maturity and calling of God. They challenged my reasoned explanations and biblical teachings on the basic doctrines of historic Christianity to see if I understood and stood on the truth and authority of the Holy Scriptures.

I was then excused from the room while members of that vicinage council asked questions of some members of that local church concerning my ministry among them thus far. The council then prayed and shared with one another their observations, reflections, and assessments in order to discern together how they would advise this local church, and how they might also advise me.

When I and the leaders of that local church were called back in to receive the report of the vicinage council, it was a very serious moment for me. I was deeply aware that I could not possibly fulfill this calling of serving the Lord Jesus and His Church without the enabling and anointing of God. I knew I must lead the Lord's Church according to His Word, and as the Holy Spirit would lead me.

Still, I remember struggling with my insecurities, wondering if I was truly called, prepared, and ready to lead a congregation of God's people. Being aware of my sinfulness and limitations, and of my youth and relative inexperience, I wrestled and wondered. The leaders of that congregation were prepared to hear, and I needed to hear what that seasoned and prayerful vicinage council would now tell us.

They had much to say that day, but the line that still rings in my ears and heart came from Rev. George Buhl, a respected and seasoned local church pastor. Rev. Buhl had held various leadership positions regionally and nationally in our biblical and congregational faith group, including serving for three years as our president.

I recall Pastor Buhl facing the group of leaders from that local church. He paused for a moment, and then said, "Over the years, I've participated in many vicinage councils to consider and advise a local congregation about the calling and readiness of someone to serve Jesus Christ and His Church as a pastor. I will say to you with utmost sincerity that I have never met or considered anyone who is more called and prepared to serve and lead the Church of Jesus Christ than is this young man."

I was astounded that day and was moved to tears. Our adversary had been deceptive toward me and is deceptive toward everyone. Jesus described the devil, saying, *He has always hated the truth, because there is no truth in him. When he lies, it is consistent with his character; for he is a liar and the father of lies* (John 8:44).

I have observed and experienced that the devil continually aims to discourage and dissuade the people of God. The devil lies to us that we have not really heard God's call, or that we are not up to this task, or that we are unworthy and incapable of living this life, or that everything we have come to believe in Jesus is not true. But Jesus says otherwise.

Jesus promises to be with us always and to equip us for whatever He calls us to do. Writing from a prison cell to the local church that gathered in Philippi, the apostle Paul testified to the church what Christ had taught him through so many challenges. Paul's affirmation speaks to me and to all who are called into service by the Lord: *I can do everything through Christ, who gives me strength* (Philippians 4:13). I'll say it again. Say it with me: "Whatever God calls me to do, He always equips me to do it."

As the young pastor of that local church, I was very blessed to be reminded that Jesus Christ had in fact called me. And because God has so clearly spoken through His inspired Word, I understood and determined then, and it has been made clear to me throughout my lifetime, that I must always aim to know, live, teach, and lead according to the timeless principles that God has revealed in the Bible, His inspired and holy Word.

My life of following Jesus and leading in His Church has taken me along unexpected paths. At every juncture I have known that my Lord is leading me. I have been blessed to serve Jesus in various positions of ministry leadership, including three times as pastor or senior pastor of a local church.

Very surprisingly to me, the Lord Jesus also led me to serve as a United States Navy Chaplain. In this ministry I worked alongside and cared for people of various religious perspectives, and many with no professed faith at all.

I also ministered with Christians from many denominational perspectives, theological understandings, and liturgical practices. In all cases I was blessed to answer the Lord's call for my life – to demonstrate God's love, declare God's truth, and point people toward Jesus Christ, who is Savior and Lord of all, and head of His body, the church.

Three times I served as a local church pastor (1980-1989, 1996-2003, and 2016-2018), and for twenty-seven years I served as a military chaplain on active duty or in the Reserves (1989-2016). For eight years I was called and blessed by Jesus to serve in a national leadership role as Conference Minister of the Conservative Congregational Christian Conference (2003-2011).

In all of these ministry leadership roles, I was blessed to learn firsthand that the only way I could carry out my role is by leaning on Jesus, trusting in His Word, and living according to biblical truths. I have observed that whenever the Bible is regarded as our supreme standard for faith and practice, and when basic biblical principles are known and lived, then blessings are in store for the church and the people of God. I have also observed that whenever biblical principles are unknown or are not being applied, then the local church and the people of God will be unable to experience God's best.

And so, after a lifetime of faith in Jesus Christ and love for Him and His Church, I have been brought to this place of writing about some basic principles of local church governance for being and leading local churches biblically. Remember again the emphatic words of Jesus as recorded in Luke 12:48. He said then and says to us now, *When someone has been entrusted with much, even more will be required.*

Well, I have been given so much! I fully expect that if you think about this in the context of God's amazing grace, you will see that you also have been given much. The question then for all of us is, "What now, Lord?"

In my life review thus far, in the name of Jesus I have visited and served in every state in the United States of America. I have served my Lord on many islands and on every continent except Antarctica. I have ministered in hundreds of local churches across the USA and in some other nations. Having had a leadership role in the World Evangelical Congregational Fellowship (WECF), I have had blessed connections with brothers and sisters in Christ, and local churches and leaders, in many countries and cultures. I do not say this to boast, but to give God the glory.

In living the life of ministry to which Jesus Christ called me, and in loving and serving His Church, I have reflected much on timeless truths that apply in all local churches and in every cultural context. I have observed firsthand that whenever these biblical principles are known and applied by leaders of the local church, and then by the congregation as a whole, the blessings and promises of God are known.

Regrettably, I have also observed that whenever these biblical principles are unknown or are ignored by local church leaders and members, then conflict and trouble come. And so, in God's loving mercy, the Lord of the Church, even of every local church, calls us to a refresher course about basic biblical principles of local church governance for being and leading local churches.

We have very good reasons to rejoice today. The biblical principles we will consider are as relevant and helpful in local church governance today as they have been since the earliest days of the Christian Church.

Introduction

Biblical Pictures: Pages of God's Blueprints for His Church

We will start with two metaphors that together can help us see what God intends as we labor to plant and build local churches for the honor and glory of the Lord Jesus Christ. The two metaphors are photos and blueprints.

Do you, as I do, take photos of places, people, and things that you wish to remember? On a recent trip overseas, I took hundreds of photos. I did it for my own sake to refresh memories later, and because I wanted to share with others some of what I had seen, experienced, and learned.

The Bible contains a number of snapshots that can show us how Jesus sees His Church and what He intends for His local churches to be. The Lord Himself has given us these photos so we will see what He sees concerning His Church, and so we can use these images to show others what it looks like to build Christ's local churches as He intends.

A second metaphor involves pages from the architect's blueprints. This is what the pages of the Bible are for us. When a new building is under construction, the builders may often refer to the architect's blueprints to know the measurements and design intended by the architect. Without blueprints, and without builders referring to them often, the building will not become what it was meant to be.

For those who would build the Church of Jesus Christ, Jesus provides all the necessary guidance and tools. Our responsibility as leaders of His local churches is to continually reference God's biblical blueprints to ensure we are constructing it according to His design. As we labor for Jesus in His Church, we keep returning to the Bible, asking God to help us see and follow the pattern He has laid out for us.

We will look at six biblical photos that show us how Jesus views His Church. These serve as our Lord's blueprints for our local church governance, and are applicable no matter the generation, nation, culture, meeting place, denomination, or structure.

We will then consider six contrived images that illustrate what the Church is not. These are like photos that have been derived artificially. At first glance they can appear beautiful and real, but upon closer examination, we can see they are fake and deceptively made, as by photoshopping. It is important for local churches and church leaders to prayerfully and rightly discern what God's will is according to His revealed Word. This is how we can rightly distinguish between what is true and false, real and unreal, concerning God's will for His Church and for our local churches.

We will then consider three primary forms of local church governance that have emerged in Church history. Though we cannot say with complete certainty, these three patterns of local church structure may well have developed out of differing understandings of church offices mentioned in the Bible, and in writings of early church fathers before the canon of the New Testament was established.

Early church structures varied, but God the Holy Spirit drew people to faith in Jesus Christ, expanding His Church. Leaders aimed to glorify Jesus and spread His gospel of salvation by grace and through faith. This gospel was at first delivered by the apostles, who were eyewitnesses of the life, death, resurrection, and ascension of Jesus. Having received from Jesus the Great Commission, they were determined to faithfully follow Him, declaring His good news and making disciples wherever He would lead them. And so the church of Jesus Christ began spreading like wildfire.

Through the inspiration, illumination, leading, and oversight of the Holy Spirit, the Word of God was written and preserved for the sake of the church then, throughout history, and today. The gospel of Jesus Christ was confirmed then and now through signs and wonders, by the amazing grace of God in bringing people to saving faith in Jesus Christ, and through the miracle of unity in the Holy Spirit. Through all of this, Jesus Christ has been building His Church in and through many nations, cultures, languages, and expressions.

Just as the early Church was built upon the gospel of Jesus Christ, and as it was proclaimed by the anointed teaching of the apostles under the inspiration of the Holy Spirit, so must the church be built today. The local churches that we serve are to be built upon the same gospel of Jesus that was conveyed by the apostles. And so we who lead in Christ's Church must ensure that we are building this local hurch biblically.

Three primary offices were mentioned in the Koine Greek language of the New Testament, and in writings of early church leaders. Those biblical offices were *episkopos* (bishop or overseer), *presbuteros* (presbyters or elders), and *diakonos* (deacons, who, according to Acts 6, were chosen by the congregation).

Three primary forms of local church governance that emerged in early church history were episcopal, presbyterian, and congregational. We will review these three forms of governance, observing that the Church of Jesus Christ has not been exclusive to just one of these structures. Of far higher importance than the denominational or congregational structure of a local church is the church's belief and practice of some foundational principles of biblical Christianity.

We will then focus on the three primary levels of authority and responsibility that must be established in all local churches that desire to be faithful and biblical. These apply in every local church, no matter its structure or denominational affiliation. Three primary levels of authority and responsibility for every local church are headship, leadership, and membership.

We will then center on six foundational faith convictions of historic biblical Christianity. These will be emphasized in every local church that prayerfully aims to be biblical in obedience to Jesus Christ. These convictions must be settled in the hearts of church leaders in order to be modeled and taught to all disciples of Jesus who are part of that local church. These foundational truths about the good news of Jesus Christ will be the primary message and witness of the local church.

After we have examined these foundational faith convictions for local churches, we will conclude with four cautions of carefulness for all local church leaders and churches. These are essentially biblical warnings of things to prayerfully avoid in the local church. We know that ultimately this church belongs to Jesus Christ, who has entrusted the church to us under His supreme authority and headship.

Whenever God speaks to His people, He always calls for response. In light of this, each section of this study includes a question or two for personal reflection or prayerful discussion.

An addendum at the end of this volume is for local churches and leaders who are practicing biblical congregationalism. History has shown that Christians who are equally committed to Jesus Christ and the authority of Scripture can differ in their views on church structures and other secondary matters. When this happens, we must remember that our Lord views His worldwide Church as one, so we must too.

Shortly before Jesus was betrayed and arrested, on the night before He laid down His life and died on the cross for our salvation, Jesus prayed for His Church. The apostle John heard and recorded Jesus's words. Jesus prayed for His Church to be one as He is one with His Father. Jesus's prayer for the Church, which encompasses all of our local churches, includes these instructive and convicting words:

> *I am praying not only for these disciples but also for all who will ever believe in me through their message. I pray that they will all be one, just as you and I are one—as you are in me, Father, and I am in you. And may they be in us so that the world will believe you sent me. I have given them the glory you gave me, so they may be one as we are one. I am in them and you are in me. May they experience such perfect unity that the world will know that you sent me and that you love them as much as you love me.* (John 17:20-23)

In light of this fervent prayer of Jesus, I am fully convinced that He does not want His Church to divide over secondary matters, which includes the matter of how local churches should be structured. This is not to suggest that such matters are unimportant, but only that in the heart of Jesus, these are not important enough for us to divide over. Having said this, biblical churches will always aim to apply biblical principles in the ways that they love and live with one another.

Because my own life and local church ministry has primarily been within the framework of biblical congregationalism, in the addendum I include a little history, along with insights that can be helpful in congregational church governance. I share a few lessons the Lord taught me in leading local churches congregationally and through leadership in a congregational denomination. I also include some insights gained in participation with the World Evangelical Congregational Fellowship which, as its name suggests, is an international family of congregational fellowships that aim to be biblical and congregational in faith and practice.

Where Is the Church of Jesus Christ?

Before opening God's Word to consider who the Church is and how local church leaders are to lead biblically, it is important to consider where the Lord's Church is on this earth. There are two clear answers to this.

First, the Church of Jesus Christ is worldwide, for Jesus came for the whole world. Jesus promised His disciples that when the Holy Spirit comes upon us, we will bring His gospel to the whole world: *But you will receive power when the Holy Spirit comes upon you. And you will be my witnesses, telling people about me everywhere—in Jerusalem, throughout Judea, in Samaria, and to the ends of the earth* (Acts 1:8).

It is good to pause here to thank God that this promise included the part of the world where we are now living. The good news of Jesus Christ was brought right here, and by God's grace you and I were called and invited to believe and receive.

It is also good for us to be praying now for the complete fulfillment of our Lord's vision and promise that His Church will continue expanding to reach the whole world. Let the churches be praying toward that end for the parts of our own nations and regions, and for all places around the globe where there is not yet a faithful witness for people to hear and receive the true gospel of Jesus Christ.

This brings us to a second biblical answer to the question of where the Church is. Not only is it worldwide, but the Church of Jesus Christ is always local. Much of the New Testament is addressed to local churches, with guidance on being and leading the Church in the places where God plants us.

The Church of Jesus Christ is local. It is wherever He has called us to live and serve, wherever followers of Jesus gather across this world, whether the local church consists of many or only a few. If our local church is just getting started, or if our local church is small, it is helpful to remember our Lord's specific promise that applies no matter what the size of the crowd is. Jesus said, *Where two or three gather together as my followers, I am there among them* (Matthew 18:20).

And so, with both the worldwide Church and our local church in mind, let us open the Scriptures with a desire to live and lead according to God's plans. Toward that end we will begin with the two metaphors introduced earlier, which can help us see what God intends for those who are aiming to build local churches for the honor and glory of Jesus Christ. The two metaphors we will use are photos and blueprints.

Chapter 1

What the Church Truly Is

Biblical Pictures – Pages of God's Blueprints for His Church

Do you take a lot of photos like I do? I just opened my smartphone to see how many photos are saved on it. Today it says there are 5,302 photos and 475 videos. This may be more or less than the photos you have saved, but our common reasons for taking and keeping photos are primarily two: (1) we desire to remember, and (2) we want to share with somebody else what we have seen, learned, or experienced.

This is why God has included in His Word the beautiful pictures of His Church. God wants us to see what He sees, not forgetting the beauty. He wants us to show and tell others some of what God has shown us, including showing the congregations He has called us to love and serve what He intends for His Church.

Have you ever been involved in planning or constructing a new building, or watching a new building under construction? Builders will keep referring to the blueprints to ensure that the building is being formed according to the architect's plans. This is why local churches and church leaders must often refer to God's blueprints that are found in the Bible. We desire to ensure that we are building Christ's Church according to His will.

We will look at six biblical pictures, or pages, of God's blueprints for His Church. As we examine these, we will see some of what Jesus intends His local churches to look like and be like. We will receive guidance from the Lord Jesus on building His Church as He intends.

1. The Church is the Body of Jesus Christ. Because we all live in human bodies, we understand this image. We know what it means for the parts of our body to function together as one body for the common good. We know that when one part of our body experiences pain, the whole body is impacted. We also grasp that with our physical body, there is only one head, and it is the head that determines where and when the body will go and what the body will do. So it is with the Church. The Church, including every true local church, is the Body of Jesus Christ.

This biblical photo and page of God's blueprints for His church reveal that together we are the Body of Jesus Christ. We are all connected to each other. As His Body, we desire and need to be led by our Head, even Jesus Christ. This photo shows several aspects of God's beautiful plan for His whole Church, and for every local church, including the congregation that we are called by God to lead or serve. God says to His churches: *You are the body of Christ and individually members of it* (1 Corinthians 12:27 ESV). *He [Jesus] is the head of the body, the church* (Colossians 1:18 ESV).

For personal reflection: What are some implications for you personally of the Church, even your local church, being the Body of Jesus Christ together?

For church leaders' discussion: What are some implications for you as church leaders, and for your congregation, that you are together the Body of Jesus Christ?

2. The Church is the Bride of Jesus Christ. This picture and page give us a glimpse of our Lord's love, devotion, and commitment to us, His church. It also speaks of His desire for His bride to only have eyes for Him – deeply loving Him, being devoted and committed to loving Jesus for all our days and forever. This is how Jesus loves us, and He desires a church that loves Him like a faithful and devoted bride.

It seems remarkable to me that my wife Helen and I are approaching the fiftieth anniversary of our married life together. We are incredibly grateful for the life we have experienced with each other, through so many wonderful joys, as well as through struggles and challenges. We have shared easy times and difficult times. We have walked together through seasons of strong faith and certainty, and admittedly through some seasons of painful doubt and uncertainty. We have walked together through plenty and want, strength and weakness, good health and devastating illness, great joy and deep sorrow. Looking back over fifty years together, Helen and I celebrate with praise to God and thankfulness to God and each other that because of Jesus, our love has endured through it all.

We are thankful that when we were young, the Lord Jesus led us both to commit ourselves first to God and then to each other. We are blessed to have lived together in a lifelong covenant of love. As we have leaned together upon Jesus, walking with Him in faith, He has equipped us with all we have needed.

I carry in my memory a stunning photo that I will never forget. As I stood near the altar on our wedding day, looking down the aisle in that church sanctuary, I beheld my beautiful bride. There she was, on the arm of her father, who was bringing her to me. She was so beautiful. I will always remember and treasure the love and joy I had that day. My bride had made herself ready, and there she was.

As I contemplate that beautiful picture imprinted forever in my memory, I think too of the deep love Jesus Christ has for us, His church, His beloved bride! Can we begin to fathom how deep His love is for us? The Bible says this about the love Jesus has for His bride: *Christ loved the church. He gave up his life for her to make her holy and clean, washed by the cleansing of God's word. He did this to present her to himself as a glorious church without a spot or wrinkle or any other blemish. Instead, she will be holy and without fault* (Ephesians 5:25-27).

When Helen and I married, we declared in faith to each other and to all who would hear that the covenant we were making with one another was to be together "until death separates us." That has been our assurance through the years, and neither of us has ever doubted that our spouse loves us or would remain with us. We have a similar assurance in the eternal covenant of love between the Lord and His Church.

This beautiful picture and page of God's blueprints for building His Church shows a covenant of eternal love that will never end, but is for time and for eternity. This is a biblical promise: *Let us be glad and rejoice, and let us give honor to him. For the time has come for the wedding feast of the Lamb, and his bride has prepared herself* (Revelation 19:7). *And the angel said to me, . . . "Blessed are those who are invited to the marriage feast of the Lamb"* (Revelation 19:9).

For personal reflection: What are some implications for you personally of the Church, including your local church, being the Bride of Jesus Christ?

For local church leaders' discussion: What are implications for you as church leaders, and for your congregation, that you are together the bride of Jesus Christ?

3. The Church is the Family of God in Jesus Christ. Jesus taught that all who believe in Him, having received Him in faith and are thus following Him now, are God's own children. How precious is that thought! So, as we grow up spiritually in a personal relationship with Jesus, we increasingly learn that we can approach God in faith at any time.

We can do this because God has adopted us into His family as His children. God invites and welcomes us who are His children to come near, like a loving father does for his children. God has made this clear in the blueprints of the Bible.

> *Even before he made the world, God loved us and chose us in Christ to be holy and without fault in his eyes. God decided in advance to adopt us into his own family by bringing us to himself through Jesus Christ. This is what he wanted to do, and it gave him great pleasure. So we praise God for the glorious grace he has poured out on us who belong to his dear Son. He is so rich in kindness and grace that he purchased our freedom with the blood of his Son and forgave our sins. He has showered his kindness on us, along with all wisdom and understanding.* (Ephesians 1:4-8)

God has made an invitation and promise to all who are His Church and therefore part of His family: *Come close to God, and God will come close to you. Wash your hands, you sinners; purify your hearts, for your loyalty is divided between God and the world* (James 4:8).

So yes, this wonderful truth that we are God's own children means that whenever local churches come together, we are gathering as God's own family. God loves His children very much and does not want any of them to feel alone or to live in isolation. God calls and equips His family to love and live together as brothers and sisters. God does not want or expect us to do this in our own efforts or natural abilities, for like obstinate children, when left to ourselves we are selfishly prone to fight and squabble.

But God, who loves us so and is truly with us always, helps us love one another because we are His family together. To the local church gathered in Ephesus, Paul gave this reminder, which God now gives to us and to our local churches: *You are no longer strangers and aliens, but you are fellow citizens with the saints and members of the household of God* (Ephesians 2:19 ESV).

This means that every person who is part of your local church through faith in Jesus is with you in God's family. Do you see them as your family? Do you look for ways to encourage, welcome, and bless members of your family, even those who are different from you or with whom you might disagree on some things? Our Lord intends for our local churches to live, love, and serve one another as His family and to bring His love to this world.

In chapter two of Paul's letter to the church in Ephesus, Paul reminded the Ephesian Christians that no one has any basis for spiritual pride. None of us can take personal credit for our salvation, for we did nothing to earn it.

Verses 8-9 speak of the absolute necessity of God's grace to us and also of our response of faith. Paul wrote, *God saved you by his grace when you believed. And you can't take credit for this; it is a gift from God. Salvation is not a reward for the good things we have done, so none of us can boast about it.* The next verse adds another crucial message for local churches: *For we are God's masterpiece. He has created us anew in Christ Jesus, so we can do the good things he planned for us long ago* (Ephesians 2:10). Here the Holy Spirit reveals to God's family that God has prepared divine appointments for each and all of us who are part of His Church family. This message is for you personally and for your local congregation and every member of it.

In light of God's amazing love and grace to us, what is our individual and collective responsibility? Surely it includes our desiring and allowing the Holy Spirit to lead us to recognize and respond to every divine appointment God prepares for us to do. This is our duty and privilege as local churches in Jesus Christ, and as God's own children, for we are God's loved family.

I could share many testimonies of blessings I have known and miracles I have witnessed while living this way. In later years, when at times I have grieved because I could no longer serve in ways I previously served, my Lord has reminded me that as long as I breathe, He has good works *prepared beforehand* (Ephesians 2:10 ESV) for me to do.

Divine appointments will not stop for local churches, nor for any who are God's children through faith in Jesus until He calls us home and we hear Him say, *Well done, my good and faithful servant* (Matthew 25:23). Hearing those words on that day implies our faithfulness in these days.

When the Lord's church members offer themselves to Him as His prayerfully available children, He will direct their steps and make His direction clear. I will illustrate this with a personal example that occurred in my walk with Jesus the week that I wrote this chapter. Having learned to trust God to direct my steps in regard to the divine appointments He has prepared for me, I was not troubled on the day when an expected event for me was suddenly canceled. I had been in the hospital several hours preparing for a medical procedure. I was lying in a hospital bed and was being attended to by a nurse who was inserting an IV into my arm just before I was to be rolled in for the procedure.

Suddenly I heard another nearby nurse yell, "Stop!" She then approached and announced that my scheduled procedure was postponed because the primary machine that was to be used for that procedure was malfunctioning. Although I was disappointed when I heard this news, I was not troubled, because the Holy Spirit reminded me of this biblical truth. This development, which I did not expect, was no surprise to God. I sensed that God had brought me there that day for other reasons – for divine appointments He had prepared in advance for me to do.

Two such appointments unfolded. One was a personal conversation with a nurse named Cindy, who quoted a Bible verse to me that God alone knew I needed to hear that day. A second divine appointment that day was an encounter with a man named Tim, whom I met as I departed the hospital and was walking on the path toward my car. I saw that he seemed lonely and troubled. Being available to the Lord, and recognizing this as a divine appointment, I prayerfully approached Tim. I gave the gift of time to listen to him, and I offered God's compassionate love, truth, and grace.

Nearing the end of our time together that day, as we stood beside the sidewalk that led to and from the hospital, and as people were passing by, God allowed me, as His child and on His behalf, to bring His love that day. I put my arm around Tim's shoulders as he put his arm around mine, and I prayed for him, blessing him in Jesus's name. I have no idea what enduring fruit came from that divine appointment, but I know that the Lord was working out His purpose that day, and I was blessed to be part of it. This is the blessing of seeing and responding to God's divine appointments for us.

All of us who are in God's Church can extend His love in His name to one another as family, and we can do this to all to whom God leads us. For our local churches and every member, we can learn to recognize and respond to the divine appointments that will surely come, for God has prepared them for His children.

Because our local churches are God's own household and family, our aim has to be to love one another as family, to truly care for each other, and to enjoy being together, loving one another as Jesus Christ has loved us. We can celebrate the reality that Jesus Christ has made us family for this season of time and forever. It is so good for us to remember this whenever the local church gathers, for we are family now and we will be God's family forever. *To all who believed him [Jesus] and accepted him, he gave the right to become children of God* (John 1:12). *See how very much our Father loves us, for he calls us his children, and that is what we are!* (1 John 3:1).

Because every local church is part of God's family, and because we know that Jesus Christ came for us and for the world, we who are blessed to be part of God's family through faith in Jesus share His desire that His family will grow as more people come to saving faith in Him. Like our Father in heaven, we who are His family long for more people to come to repentance, to personal faith in Jesus, and so to know the joy we know of everlasting life and love in Jesus. *The Lord isn't really being slow about his promise, as some people think. No, he is being patient for your sake. He does not want anyone to be destroyed, but wants everyone to repent* (2 Peter 3:9).

The Great Commission that Jesus Christ gave to us is for every local church. He commissions His family to take His love and truth to the world. Wherever God leads us, we can faithfully respond to the divine appointments He has prepared.

For personal reflection: What does it mean to you personally that your local church is God's own family, and that you are part of it? What is your response to the biblical concept that God has prepared divine appointments in advance for you to do?

For church leaders' discussion: What does it mean for you as church leaders, and for your congregation, that you are God's own family? What are some practical ways you can encourage your local church to live the biblical principle of faithfulness in divine appointments that God has prepared for us to do?

4. The Church is the *ekklesia* of called-out ones in Jesus Christ. In the earliest days of the Christian church, in the Koine Greek language of the New Testament, local congregations of Jesus's followers were referred to as the *ekklesia*, or the called-out ones. This is the Church.

The Church began in Jerusalem and spread out from there. Wherever there were multiple people who had received and believed the good news of Jesus Christ, and who were thus determined to love and follow Jesus, they gathered together with each other in local congregations of called-out ones. It is the same today.

But sadly, sometimes those who have been around the Church a long time may begin taking these blessings for granted. This has been true in large portions of the Western Church, where a decline in local church attendance has been seen in recent years.

Several studies have been done on this issue in various nations. In the USA, for example, there has been a marked waning in church attendance since the turn of the twenty-first century, according to surveys from various research institutions. Gallup's 2024 survey illustrated this trend, showing a precipitous decline in the number of people who say that their religious faith is very important in their life. This is reflected in a declining percentage of people who report that they attend worship services weekly (20 percent in 2024). The trend is also seen in an increasing percentage of Americans who say they seldom or never attend religious services (57 percent in 2024).[1]

Some attribute these detrimental changes to the effects of the worldwide pandemic. In 2020, churches in many lands were forced to close for a prolonged time. When these restrictions were eventually lifted, some previous attendees never returned because they had become accustomed to living without gathering with other Christ followers for worship, and they did not miss it.

This excuse for withdrawing from Christian fellowship and corporate worship shows lack of commitment to Jesus and His family. All who have heard Jesus's calling to "Follow Me," and who have said, "Yes, Lord, I will follow," will not want to quit but will want to faithfully follow Him until the end. We will discover that much like hot coals, staying hot for Jesus requires staying in the fire of Christian fellowship.

I was blessed to have been a shepherd of God's flock for many years. During those years, I sadly witnessed some people leave the church for various feeble reasons, reflecting their limited love for the Lord and their small regard for the gift of Christ's church. I have observed teenagers leave the church after getting their driver's license, starting a sport, or getting a job. Young adults may stop attending after high school, couples after marriage, and spouses after divorce. Adults may leave due to work, hobbies, conflicts with the pastor, music preferences, or other minor reasons.

In contrast to all of this, my Lord has allowed me to witness and marvel at Christians who love Jesus deeply and who profoundly treasure the gift of God that is found in sweet gatherings of *ekklesia*. I observed a particularly memorable example of this several years ago when ministering in a remote mountain village in Nepal. Getting there required many hours of climbing a steep and narrow mountain trail. When I

---

1   Gallup.com, https://news.gallup.com/poll/642548/church-attendance-declined-religious-groups.aspx, March 25, 2024, and https://news.gallup.com/poll/358364/religious-americans.aspx, March 29, 2024.

and others who were with me arrived at that village well after dark, we found that about two hundred church leaders had gathered from scattered locations across Nepal, including some who had walked for many days to get there. They were joyfully worshipping.

I later learned that several members of that local *ekklesia* lived down on the base of that mountain and trek up and down that trail every single week. Why would they do this? That *ekklesia* was the closest gathering of Christians to where they lived. The biblical teaching, fellowship, friendships, and worship they experienced in that local church was a treasure that energized and spiritually fed them. They considered their weekly climb up and down that mountain to be a trivial price to pay for such great blessings!

May God grant more of us a perspective like this so that our church members would increasingly treasure the great gift that God has given through His Church – the blessing of joining others in a local *ekklesia* of those who love Jesus, and who, like us, have been called out from this world to love and follow Him now. This treasure is certainly worth climbing high mountains for.

While visiting Greece to see a friend, Helen and I visited some of the cities that are mentioned in the New Testament where the apostle Paul once ministered. In doing this, we always opened God's Word to read Bible verses that referenced those people and places. One of those cities was Corinth, which we read about in Acts 18.

After bringing the good news of Jesus Christ to Athens, Paul journeyed on about fifty miles further to Corinth. There Jesus had prepared for him and for those whom he was going to meet a special divine appointment. There he became acquainted with a Jew named Aquila, born in Pontus, who had recently arrived from Italy with his wife, Priscilla. They had left Italy when Claudius Caesar deported all Jews from Rome. Paul lived and worked with them, for they were tentmakers, just as he was (Acts 18:1-3).

In God's grace, Paul was connected with this Christian couple. God still purposefully connects brothers and sisters in Christ in and through the *ekklesia*. Aquila and Priscilla were tentmakers like Paul was, and they were led by the Lord to combine their tentmaking businesses together. In this way, God provided for their daily needs, while giving them fellowship and encouragement. They also combined their labor in establishing the new local *ekklesia* in the city of Corinth.

Priscilla and Aquila brought Paul with them to the synagogue in Corinth, where Paul preached the good news of Jesus. Acts 18 goes on to tell of the first Christian converts in Corinth, including a gentile named Titius Justus, who lived next door to the synagogue, and a Jewish man named Crispus, who was a former leader of the synagogue. Verse 8 adds, *Many others in Corinth also heard Paul, became believers, and were baptized.* And so the local *ekklesia* was born in Corinth. As that local church grew, it remained dear to Paul, which led him to make multiple return journeys to Corinth. He also wrote the inspired letters to that local *ekklesia* that became part of our New Testament.

Hear how Paul addressed that local *ekklesia* in these letters:

> *I am writing to God's church in Corinth, to you who have been called by God to be his own holy people. He made you holy by means of Christ Jesus, just as he did for all people everywhere who call on the name of our Lord Jesus Christ, their Lord and ours.* (1 Corinthians 1:2)

> *I am writing to God's church in Corinth and to all of his holy people throughout Greece.* (2 Corinthians 1:1)

When Paul addressed the church in Corinth, he was referring to local congregations of Christians who met in that city. As mentioned earlier, the local church was referred to as the *ekklesia*, or "called-out ones," meaning those who were called out from this world by God's grace, having been made holy *by means of Christ Jesus.*

So sweet was the bond that Paul, Priscilla, and Aquila had known from having been part of that local *ekklesia* together, that many years later, Paul still remembered his dear friends fondly, so he sent them his warm personal greetings. In the same way that we fondly consider dear brothers and sisters in Christ with whom we were once in fellowship, so Paul longed for these friends with whom he once lived and loved and served in Corinth. They remained as family to him.

When Paul wrote his letter to the *ekklesia* in Rome, Priscilla and

Aquila were faithfully serving Jesus there. As Paul neared the end of his letter, he added personal greetings to these dear friends and to the local church that met in their house. Again, he referred to that local gathering of believers as the *ekklesia* – those who had been called out from this world to follow Jesus: *Give my greetings to Priscilla and Aquila, my co-workers in the ministry of Christ Jesus. In fact, they once risked their lives for me. I am thankful to them, and so are all the Gentile churches. Also give my greetings to the church [ekklesia] that meets in their home* (Romans 16:3-5).

What a gift to be with others in an *ekklesia* of God's people! Another of Paul's letters was to be circulated in the region of Galatia. As that letter was intended for the local *ekklesia* throughout that province, he began with these words: *Paul, an apostle—not from men nor through man, but through Jesus Christ and God the Father, who raised him from the dead—and all the brothers who are with me, to the churches [ekklesia] of Galatia: grace to you and peace from God our Father and the Lord Jesus Christ* (Galatians 1:1-3 ESV).

For personal reflection: What are some implications for you personally of the Church, even your local church, being an *ekklesia* of called-out ones?

For local church leaders' discussion: How could your local church even more fully treasure the gift and calling of being an *ekklesia* of called-out ones?

5. The Church is the Kingdom of God in Jesus Christ. When Jesus started His public ministry, He proclaimed, *The Kingdom of God is near!* (Mark 1:15). What did this imply? Surely it implied and implies still that the King has come and is here.

What does this biblical photo and page of God's blueprints suggest for us and our local churches? Because the church is the Kingdom of God, and because Jesus Christ is king of His great kingdom, God clearly says to all who are part of His churches and to all who would lead His churches that He is king, so we are not!

In this beautiful picture and page of God's blueprints for His churches, we can see that in God's perfect design, all local churches are under the rule and reign of Jesus. He is the supreme king of all, King of kings and Lord of lords.

Three times in the Bible, Jesus is given the title of King of kings and Lord of lords (1 Timothy 6:15; Revelation 17:14; 19:16). To be a king is to have power and sovereignty. To be the king above all other kings is to have *all* power and sovereignty. King Jesus is now and forever the omnipotent, omniscient, all-powerful, and all-knowing sovereign king of heaven and earth. King Jesus will reign over all things for all time.

This reality was established by God without input or vote by humanity. This is true whether or not you or I, the leaders of nations, peoples of this world, or adherents of this world's many religions agree or approve of it. Jesus Christ is King of kings, and He will reign forever and ever: *The seventh angel blew his trumpet, and there were loud voices shouting in heaven: "The world has now become the Kingdom of our Lord and of his Christ, and he will reign forever and ever"* (Revelation 11:15).

Though this eternal reality is already true, because of sinfulness, most of humanity has not yet believed or acknowledged that He is king of all, including of our lives. But there have been remarkable people of faith throughout history to whom God has given this special revelation of faith. From King David, for example, who was then king of Israel, we read of his beautiful confession of faith in God:

> *Then David praised the LORD in the presence of the whole assembly: "O LORD, the God of our ancestor Israel, may you be praised forever and ever! Yours, O LORD, is the greatness, the power, the glory, the victory, and the majesty. Everything in the heavens and on earth is yours, O LORD, and this is your kingdom. We adore you as the one who is over all things. Wealth and honor come from you alone, for you rule over everything. Power and might are in your hand, and at your discretion people are made great and given strength."*
> (1 Chronicles 29:10-12)

Even King Nebuchadnezzar, then ruler of the entire Babylonian Empire, came by grace to acknowledge that God was sovereign ruler of all, as described by Daniel: *I praised and worshiped the Most High and honored the one who lives forever. His rule is everlasting, and his kingdom is eternal. . . . Now I, Nebuchadnezzar, praise and glorify and honor the*

King of heaven. All his acts are just and true, and he is able to humble the proud (Daniel 4:34, 37).

So what about in our day? Who in this generation acknowledges the true King? Who now testifies that the eternal King has come and that Jesus is His name? The answer is that the Lord's Church does! The Church is the Kingdom of God in Jesus Christ, and we know it. We believe it. Therefore, members of local congregations covenant with one another to live together under Christ's righteous and supreme authority.

We who are members of the Church of Jesus Christ must remember the declaration He made just before He gave us our assignment and then ascended into heaven: *Jesus came and told his disciples, "I have been given all authority in heaven and on earth. Therefore, go and make disciples of all the nations, baptizing them in the name of the Father and the Son and the Holy Spirit. Teach these new disciples to obey all the commands I have given you. And be sure of this: I am with you always, even to the end of the age"* (Matthew 28:18-20).

The entire Church of Jesus Christ, including every local church, is under the sovereign authority of King Jesus. We know we are the Kingdom of God. So what does this mean in regard to how our local churches are to live, serve, and minister together? This means that we who lead the church must ensure that we are regarding and revering Jesus as our sovereign Lord and King. This means that members of the church will not be considering Jesus as the sort of king who will do things our way, according to our wisdom and desires, or even according to what the majority of us want or vote for.

We know this is His kingdom, not ours. Christ's intent is that in our local churches we would see ourselves individually and collectively as blessed servants of Jesus, the great King whom we adore. Though most of humanity does not yet grasp that Jesus is truly the sovereign King, He intends that in our local churches we will seize upon this truth, being extremely glad that we are together in God's kingdom for this time and for all eternity.

Jesus wants us to live with this awareness and eternal perspective in mind. Like King David who reigned over Israel about three millennia ago, like Nebuchadnezzar who reigned over Babylon about twenty-six centuries ago, and like the apostles who walked with Jesus and spread

His gospel about two millennia ago, countless people of faith in history have preceded us in loving and yielding to the King of All.

We who follow Jesus must know that a glorious day is coming when believers will be gathered before His throne from every generation, culture, nation, and local congregation. We will forever be together with King Jesus in His eternal kingdom.

Therefore, let us hang this beautiful picture and page of God's blueprints in each of our hearts and local churches. Let it hang in our hearts of faith until that glorious day comes when we will behold what Jesus revealed to the apostle John, who called himself, as we all can do, *the disciple Jesus loved* (John 13:23; 19:26; 21:7; 21:20).

John saw and described this beautiful scene:

> *I looked, and behold, a great multitude that no one could number, from every nation, from all tribes and peoples and languages, standing before the throne and before the Lamb, clothed in white robes, with palm branches in their hands, and crying out with a loud voice, "Salvation belongs to our God who sits on the throne, and to the Lamb!" And all the angels were standing around the throne and around the elders and the four living creatures, and they fell on their faces before the throne and worshiped God, saying, "Amen! Blessing and glory and wisdom and thanksgiving and honor and power and might be to our God forever and ever! Amen."* (Revelation 7:9-12 ESV)

For personal reflection: What has been your own response to the biblical assertion that Jesus Christ is now and forever King of kings? What might the effect of this realization be for you going forward?

For church leaders' discussion: What are some of the implications for your local congregation of the Church being the Kingdom of God in Jesus Christ?

6. The Church is forever one in Jesus Christ. When God looks upon His entire worldwide church, what does He see? He sees one church.

Would not God's comprehensive, all-knowing, and all-loving perspective transcend the differences between us that too readily divide us?

I am not suggesting that doctrinal truth is unimportant to God or to His Church. In fact, contrary to the confused perspective that is too common in this generation, ultimate truth is not and can never be relative. Ultimate truth is neither subject to nor determined by the opinions, preferences, or whims of the culture or of any person.

The notion that we can determine ultimate truth is the height of arrogance, taking us back to the dawn of humanity, as recorded in the book of Genesis. The first three chapters of God's Word reveal that humanity did not create God – or anything, for that matter. God created everything. *In the beginning God created the heavens and the earth* (Genesis 1:1).

Included in God's creation of all things, God created humanity: *Then God said, "Let us make man in our image, after our likeness. . . . So God created man in his own image, in the image of God he created him; male and female he created them"* (Genesis 1:26-27).

In these early portions of God's revelation to humanity, God revealed why He made us. The answer is clear in the description of God's intention before we were created. God said, *Let us make man in our image, after our likeness.* Then, after God had created humankind, we find God's revealed description of what He did: *God created man in his own image, in the image of God he created him; male and female he created them.*

God is the ultimate source of everything and of all truth, including our life and being. Yet we are easily tempted to negate this truth, presuming that we do not really need God and that we can choose to rule our own lives, determining for ourselves what will be our truth.

Acts 17 describes the scene when the apostle Paul was in the Areopagus in the city of Athens. Pluralistic men often gathered there to discuss and debate the latest opinions on mysterious matters. Like many in our day, they were of the notion that no one could know for sure what truth is; but it sure was entertaining to hear what people were thinking and to contribute their own thoughts to the debate.

The apostle's initial presentation of the gospel of Jesus to these curious yet spiritually seeking men poked some holes in their presumption that ultimate truth cannot be firmly known. They presumed that they could decide what the truth is:

So Paul, standing before the council, addressed them as follows: "Men of Athens, I notice that you are very religious in every way, for as I was walking along I saw your many shrines. And one of your altars had this inscription on it: 'To an Unknown God.' This God, whom you worship without knowing, is the one I'm telling you about.

"He is the God who made the world and everything in it. Since he is Lord of heaven and earth, he doesn't live in manmade temples, and human hands can't serve his needs—for he has no needs. He himself gives life and breath to everything, and he satisfies every need. From one man he created all the nations throughout the whole earth. He decided beforehand when they should rise and fall, and he determined their boundaries.

"His purpose was for the nations to seek after God and perhaps feel their way toward him and find him—though he is not far from any one of us. For in him we live and move and exist. As some of your own poets have said, 'We are his offspring.' And since this is true, we shouldn't think of God as an idol designed by craftsmen from gold or silver or stone.

"God overlooked people's ignorance about these things in earlier times, but now he commands everyone everywhere to repent of their sins and turn to him. For he has set a day for judging the world with justice by the man he has appointed, and he proved to everyone who this is by raising him from the dead." (Acts 17:22-31)

The Lord's message through Paul in Athens reflects the message Christ desires to proclaim through His Church today. Paul was asserting the wonderful news that their long-held notion that truth is somehow relative and would always remain so was a false assertion, for their "unknown God" had revealed Himself in Jesus.

Paul also affirmed a timeless truth that has been declared since the dawn of human history. To his Greek audience, Paul quoted a Greek poet who had expressed a biblical truth that God has been revealing since humanity began: *For in Him we live and move and exist. As some of your own poets have said, "We are his offspring"* (Acts 17:28).

The division and confusion that have separated humanity has its roots in chapters two and three of Genesis, which is the first book of the Torah and Bible. The Hebrew name given to this first book means "in the beginning," and the actual name, "Genesis," comes from the Greek word meaning "origin." Chapter two of Genesis reveals that God's desire for humanity is to live in a personal relationship and intimate fellowship with Him, as was enjoyed in the beautiful garden of Eden. There God and humanity lived together in personal fellowship with one another, which was and still is the essential reason God created us in His own image.

Another primary truth that originates from our eternal Creator was and is that He is God, and we are not. In the garden, where humanity lived in a right relationship with our Creator, the Lord said to Adam, *You may freely eat the fruit of every tree in the garden—except the tree of the knowledge of good and evil. If you eat its fruit, you are sure to die* (Genesis 2:16-17).

God's truth is determined by God, not by those whom He has made. God's truth is not subject to or dependent on preferred outcomes and limited understandings of people. Ultimate truth does not originate from us. It comes from God. We are blessed to experience the fullness of God's best for us by living in a right relationship with God and each other through faith in Jesus Christ. The responsibility and privilege of the Church is to hear, believe, and live by the truth God has revealed.

Yet since very early in human history, people have chosen and vainly attempted to usurp God's throne and to assume His place as arbiters of truth. This was Satan's first temptation to humankind in the garden of Eden, as is told in Genesis 3. Knowing the truth of what God had said, the devil tempted Eve and Adam, and all of their descendants, to doubt, disbelieve, disregard, and disobey God's truth. Listening to the devil's lies starts with the temptation to disbelieve God.

One day Satan asked the woman, *Did God really say you must not eat the fruit from any of the trees in the garden?* (Genesis 3:1). Eve knew what

God had said, for she quoted His words, but she was open to doubting God, to determine herself what is good and evil and what is truth. *"Of course we may eat fruit from the trees in the garden," the woman replied. "It's only the fruit from the tree in the middle of the garden that we are not allowed to eat. God said, 'You must not eat it or even touch it; if you do, you will die'"* (Genesis 3:2-3).

Then came the first of Satan's lies to humanity: *"You won't die!" the serpent replied to the woman. "God knows that your eyes will be opened as soon as you eat it, and you will be like God, knowing both good and evil"* (Genesis 3:4-5).

As Adam and Eve and all of humanity since then have sinned, we all face the painful consequences of sin, including spiritual death and separation from the Holy One, just as God forewarned (Genesis 2:17). Our sin also results in painful division and distance from each other, as has been evidenced in so many ways.

The aching brokenness of divorce and abuse, crimes of hatred and inhumanity against one another, civil wars and wars between nations – these are horrific consequences of sin. These effects of sin were foreshadowed in Adam and Eve's hiding from God and from each other, and in their casting blame for the mess they were in. And so humanity has long been divided from God and from each other. The consequences of this have been horrendous, filling this world with hatred and rage, greed and injustice, and malice and murder, which were vividly evidenced early when the very first human child, Cain, killed his own brother, Abel.

All divisions among humankind are ultimately consequences of our sinful choice to rule our own lives and to be the ultimate deciders of what is true. In His Word, God clearly defines the main problem that faces humanity: *Everyone has sinned; we all fall short of God's glorious standard* (Romans 3:23). Yet in such amazing love for sinful humanity, God promised to provide a Savior, and at the right time God sent into humanity His one and only Son, the incarnate Lord Jesus Christ, to make for us a way where there was no other way.

This is how God loved the world: He gave his one and only Son, so that everyone who believes in him will not perish but have eternal life. God sent his Son into the world not to judge the world, but to save the world through him (John 3:16-17). The gospel of Jesus Christ, which is the message of all local churches, is this: *The wages of sin is death, but the free gift of God is eternal life through Christ Jesus our Lord* (Romans 6:23).

As the church experiences and declares this wonderful message of hope and everlasting life through faith in Jesus, our Lord would have us do it with God's perspective in mind – of restoration and unity with God and with one another. And so our Lord brings us back to His original blueprint for humanity – that we would be one, as God is one, fully united with God and each other.

Because we have lived our whole lives in a divided world, we can too easily bring this perspective into the Church. We can too easily accept the divisions that are between people who are different from one another. When this happens, our churches are reflecting the world more than we are reflecting Jesus.

What are some differences that divide the Church of Jesus Christ? Divisions have occurred due to different understandings on a host of theological matters, many of which are not central to the gospel of Jesus. Even more, the Church is divided by differing languages, cultures, nations, national origins, rulers, races, genders, castes, social statuses, liturgies, worship styles, music expressions, Bible translations, leadership structures, personal preferences, and denominational distinctives. When we look at the Church of Jesus Christ, we can too easily focus on our differences.

But as the Lord Jesus Christ sees His Church, does He see it like this? Does Jesus view His Church as divided by our differences because of sin? No. The perfect sacrifice of Jesus Christ, the Lamb of God, has defeated the sin that divides us, restoring us to a right relationship with God, and so also to bring peace and restoration in our relationships with one another that were previously strained and broken. *For Christ himself has brought peace to us. He united Jews and Gentiles into one people when, in his own body on the cross, he broke down the wall of hostility that separated us* (Ephesians 2:14).

God's blueprint for His church is that we are no longer divided by our differences. God's blueprint shows that He sees His Church as one in Christ. God would have us live like this with one another. Just as a body or a bride cannot be divided, neither can a local church. May God help us live with one another as one in Christ. *There is one body and one Spirit, just as you have been called to one glorious hope for the future. There is one Lord, one faith, one baptism, one God and Father of all, who is over all, in all, and living through all* (Ephesians 4:4-6). The word "one" is used seven times in these verses, telling us that Jesus sees His Church united as one. This means that our various local churches truly are connected with all Christians, wherever gathered, both nearby and around the world.

Though this may not be the way we have been seeing the Lord's Church, Jesus calls us to remember once again that we are not the authors of truth. God is, and as God sees His Church as one, we can know that it is true no matter the diversity of our cultures, denominations, and church structures. As long as the good news of Jesus Christ is being proclaimed and believed, including the truth that salvation is by God's grace alone and through faith in Jesus, we can know with certainty that God sees us as brothers and sisters with one another in Christ Jesus.

God's blueprints show that He intends for all local churches to seek and enjoy fellowship and shared ministry with other congregations of Christians, both locally and around the world, even with those who are very different from us. *To the church of God that is in Corinth, to those sanctified in Christ Jesus, called to be saints together with all those who in every place call upon the name of our Lord Jesus Christ, both their Lord and ours* (1 Corinthians 1:2 ESV).

> *They sang a new song with these words: "You are worthy to take the scroll and break its seals and open it. For you were slaughtered, and your blood has ransomed people for God from every tribe and language and people and nation. And you have caused them to become a Kingdom of priests for our God. And they will reign on the earth"* (Revelation 5:9-10).

In God's written Word, the Bible, God says that His Church is united as one now and that we will be one forever in heaven. Our Lord wants His churches to live this way now, glorifying God and blessing one another as we share His vision of a Church that is one. To the Lord Jesus, His Church is forever united across time, nations, cultures, locations, denominations, and our differences.

For personal reflection: What has been and what is going to be your response to the assertion that the Church of Jesus Christ truly is united as one, and will be so forever?

For local church leaders' discussion: What are some of the implications for your local church that, despite so many differences that have divided us, the Church of Jesus Christ is truly united as one in God's eyes?

Review: In this chapter, we have considered six biblical pictures and pages of God's blueprints for building His Church:

- The Church is the Body of Jesus Christ.

- The Church is the Bride of Jesus Christ.

- The Church is the Family of God in Jesus Christ.

- The Church is the *ekklesia* of called-out ones in Jesus Christ.

- The Church is the Kingdom of God in Jesus Christ.

- The Church is forever one in Jesus Christ.

Chapter 2

Contrived Images of What the Church Is Not

Artificial Intelligence

Not only is it important to review what the Bible says the Church is, it is also beneficial for biblical Christians to be reminded of what the Church is not. We will now look at six images that can fool some people, because these images pretend to show what the Church is. But these are manipulated photos, created as though by artificial intelligence (AI), intended to deceive. They are contrived images that illustrate what the biblical Church is not.

1. The church is not a building. For too many people, whenever a local church is referred to, they mean the building or place where Christians gather and worship happens. But the church is not a building. Various sorts of buildings are constructed of assorted sizes, designs, and degrees of simplicity or ornateness, all of which are called churches. But no such buildings are ever mentioned in the Bible, nor in the writings of the early Church.

Every biblical reference to the Church or local churches concerns the people of God, not any specific building in which they meet. Once again, in the original Koine Greek language of the New Testament, the word for "church" is *ekklesia*, or "called-out ones." This refers to the people who were called out from this world to follow Jesus.

Biblically, the local church is the people who are called out from this world into faith and a relationship with Jesus. Having heard, believed, and received Jesus as Savior and Lord. These are those who have answered His call to follow Him now, and to do so with others who also love and follow Him.

A local church is made up of people who gather with each other as called-out ones to love, follow, and serve Jesus together. The location where God's people gather is not the church. The reason for our being and for our gathering together is not to build and maintain a beautiful building, whether a magnificent cathedral or a simple structure made of mud, wood, or concrete. The church is made up of the people of God who are indwelled by the Holy Spirit and united together in faith under the headship of Jesus.

This is not to suggest that meeting places are not helpful or necessary, but local churches, church leaders, and all who would follow Jesus must be very careful to never accept the notion that a property or building is the highest priority. We are to carefully avoid devoting more of our limited time, focus, and resources on obtaining, improving, and maintaining the building where we meet than we are on growing deeper in our relationship with Jesus, making disciples for Him, and leaving a kingdom impact in this world through ministries of Christian love and truth.

Though we may sometimes refer to the place where we gather as the church, the building is not itself the church. It is simply the place where people of the local church gather in Jesus's name. Members of local churches who are aiming to be biblical in ministry and focus will thus prayerfully avoid prioritizing the property where God's people gather above the people of God who gather there.

Our higher focus must always be on our calling and privilege to be the living and breathing Church of Jesus Christ in our local community, and wherever our Lord may send us. Biblical local churches are again reminded that *all of you together are Christ's body, and each of you is a part of it* (1 Corinthians 12:27).

For personal reflection: What are some implications for you personally knowing that the people make up the true Church of Jesus Christ and are far more important to Him than any properties or buildings?

For local church leaders' discussion: What are some implications for your local congregation that, biblically speaking, the place you gather is not the Church?

2. The Church is not an imitator of the world. We must be careful that in our desire to be attractive to people of this world, we do not find ourselves being imitators of this world. Our desire cannot be to be like this world, for that is not what attracts people to Jesus. The attraction of the Church is that we are different from this world, for we are reflecting and representing the one who is not of this world, but who came to save it.

When Jesus stood before Pontius Pilate, who was then the Roman governor of Judea, Jesus knew that humanly speaking, this governor had authority to set Him free or sentence Him to die. Jesus heard this unruly mob clamoring for His death, and He knew that Pilate could be easily persuaded. So when Pilate asked Jesus, *Are you the king of the Jews?* (John 18:33), Jesus knew that His answer would lead to Pilate ordering His crucifixion. But Jesus was in control here. His life was not being taken from Him against His will. Jesus was willingly laying down His life to atone for our sins and for the sins of this world.

So to Pontius Pilate, Jesus answered, *My Kingdom is not an earthly kingdom. If it were, my followers would fight to keep me from being handed over to the Jewish leaders. But my Kingdom is not of this world* (John 18:36). Because the kingdom of Jesus Christ is not an earthly kingdom, the primary focus of His Church, including every local church, cannot be on the things of this earth. Our focus must be on things that are above, in the kingdom of our Lord. Shortly before His encounter with Pilate, as Jesus was teaching His disciples who would become pillars in establishing His Church, He said to them (and now to us), *The world would love you as one of its own if you belonged to it, but you are no longer part of the world. I chose you to come out of the world, so it hates you* (John 15:19).

It might seem strange that Jesus said we are not of this world. When He described us in this way, He was not referring to any images of aliens from other planets, as some may vainly imagine. He is clearly saying to His Church that we are to stand apart from this world, to be a light for Him.

The apostle Paul had much opportunity to reflect on these things, as he was imprisoned on several occasions because of his devotion to Jesus. This afforded Paul much quiet time to pray and carefully listen to what the Holy Spirit was saying to him and to the churches. During one imprisonment, the apostle wrote to the local church in the city of Philippi. Paul gave words of encouragement to the church not to do the things the world was doing, or to love the things the world loves, but to be different from this world; for after all, we are not of this world. And so Paul included this in his final instructions: *And now, dear brothers and sisters, one final thing. Fix your thoughts on what is true, and honorable, and right, and pure, and lovely, and admirable. Think about things that are excellent and worthy of praise* (Philippians 4:8).

Paul knew very well that like our Savior, Jesus, whom we love and serve and whose kingdom is not of this world, we too are not of this world. And so our local churches are called to think and act differently from the world around us. We are called to be like mirrors that reflect the light of God's eternal kingdom, whose sovereign ruler is Jesus. Our churches are to demonstrate His character in this world and live by His priorities, the greatest of which is to love.

Being different from this world, like Jesus, and like the apostle Paul and other faithful servants of God who have gone before us, and being unlike this world, we will lay down our lives for the Lord. His priorities will be our priorities.

The Church of Jesus Christ is not an imitator of the world. The Church is to be unlike the world that is around us, having different values and priorities and a different message. Biblical local churches must understand that their lasting, true citizenship and ultimate loyalties are not here, but are with Jesus. Jesus had this principle in mind when He prayed to His Father shortly before being arrested, which He knew would lead to His suffering and dying in our place on the cross:

> *I have given them your word. And the world hates them because they do not belong to the world, just as I do not belong to the world. I'm not asking you to take them out of the world, but to keep them safe from the evil one. They do not belong to this world any more than I do. Make them holy by your truth; teach them your word, which is truth.* (John 17:14-17)

The apostle Paul said it very clearly to the local church in Philippi, and the Holy Spirit now speaks this to us and to our local churches: *But we are citizens of heaven, where the Lord Jesus Christ lives. And we are eagerly waiting for him to return as our Savior* (Philippians 3:20).

Through the apostle Paul, our Lord gave this exhortation to the local church in the city of Colossae, and now to the local churches in our communities: *Since you have been raised to new life with Christ, set your sights on the realities of heaven, where Christ sits in the place of honor at God's right hand. Think about the things of heaven, not the things of earth* (Colossians 3:1-2).

For personal reflection: What are some implications for you personally knowing that the people make up the true Church of Jesus Christ, and thus are far more important to Him than properties or buildings?

For local church leaders' discussion: How is your local church different from this world, and how can the church show these contrasts in ways that can attract people to Jesus? What are some implications for your local church that, biblically speaking, the Church is not an imitator of the world?

3. The Church is not a club for similar people. In this world there are many opportunities for like-minded people to gather together. Similar ages, cultures, ethnicities, hobbies, interests, livelihoods, lifestyles, political and religious views, and other commonalities can draw us together. But our Lord's Church is not like that. Every local church is part of the global Church of Christ and is to reflect His love by reaching out in our communities and beyond, welcoming in Jesus's name any and all who will come.

When the makeup of a local church is wholly or primarily homogeneous, the church may only be attractive to people like us. This is especially troublesome if that congregation is satisfied with homogeneity. This is a real problem, for it indicates that this local church does not reflect the Lord's vision of gathering a diverse people, all of whom have been drawn out from the world into forgiveness, everlasting life, and fellowship with Jesus Christ and His Church.

Although it is human nature for us to be more comfortable with people who are like us, we cannot allow this preference to be our practice. Jesus desires us to become like Him, reaching out to invite and welcome all who will come, even those whose outward appearance might suggest to us that they would never consider Him. He desires His church to include the diversity of His harvest field, reflecting His promise of our eternal future in heaven.

It is good when local churches are pursuing this aim by prayerfully noticing those who live nearby who are different from them, yet for whom Christ died. Then they should ask the Lord to show them how they can reach out to these people with the love of God. Because we know that God loves them even as He loves us, it is good for local churches and church leaders to prayerfully strategize how they could show God's love to people who are different from them, and who are now apart from Christ. May our goal as local churches be for Jesus to lead us in reaching out in His name with His good news. *All who have been united with Christ in baptism have put on Christ, like putting on new clothes. There is no longer Jew or Gentile, slave or free, male and female. For you are all one in Christ Jesus* (Galatians 3:27-28).

May our churches find motivation in this beautiful picture of what our Lord has promised will be when we are at last together before His throne:

> *I saw a vast crowd, too great to count, from every nation*
> *and tribe and people and language, standing in front of*
> *the throne and before the Lamb. They were clothed in*
> *white robes and held palm branches in their hands. And*
> *they were shouting with a great roar, "Salvation comes*
> *from our God who sits on the throne and from the Lamb!"*
> (Revelation 7:9-10)

For personal reflection: What friends and acquaintances do you have among people who are very different from you? How do you show them Christ's love?

For local church leaders' discussion: What are some implications for your local church that, biblically speaking, you are not just open for people who are similar to you? What peoples in your area are different from you, and what are some ways your local church might show them Jesus's love?

4. The Church is not about satisfying ourselves or pleasing others.
This is a false image, intended to deceive. The purpose of a local church is not to make you happy or to please others. Of course, when the church is pleasing to Jesus, many will be satisfied, even beyond their dreams. But the reasons for their pleasure will not be because their own desires have all been met. It will be because Jesus Christ is exalted, His truth is spoken and lived, and His will is being done.

In what many New Testament scholars believe was the first epistle written by the apostle Paul, this matter was addressed. Paul exhorted the local church in Thessalonica with words that still speak to churches. He said, *Our purpose is to please God, not people. He alone examines the motives of our hearts* (1 Thessalonians 2:4). In other words, the church lives to please God, not ourselves or anyone else. May the worshipful aim of our local churches always be to discern and do God's will, pleasing Him with all we are and have, in our words and actions, and even in the motivations of our hearts. May our local churches be about glorifying God.

This theme was also emphasized in Paul's letter to the local church that gathered in the city of Colossae: *Let the message about Christ, in all its richness, fill your lives. Teach and counsel each other with all the wisdom he gives. Sing psalms and hymns and spiritual songs to God with thankful hearts. And whatever you do or say, do it as a representative of the Lord Jesus, giving thanks through him to God the Father* (Colossians 3:16-17).

The ultimate aim of the church is to please and glorify the Lord Jesus Christ. For the church collectively and for Christians personally, nothing is more important than this. This is living a lifestyle of worship. Worship is so much more than the songs we sing when the church gathers together. Church services can certainly be worshipful, even offering us a taste of heaven, but let us always remember that we who follow Jesus Christ are called and privileged to worship God continually as our way of life. This is preparation for the glories of heaven.

So may our aim be that everything the local church is and does will be pleasing and honoring to God. Let our aim not be to please ourselves or someone else. We will undoubtedly be pleased, for Christ is the head of His Church, and no one satisfies like Jesus. But ultimate satisfaction only happens in the local church to the extent that we are glorifying God, pleasing Him in who we are and what we do.

We might well refer to our local church as "my church" or "our church" in the sense that this is the local fellowship of God's family of which we are blessed to be a part, but every local church and its members must acknowledge that this church does not belong to us. Rather, we belong to Jesus.

The primary personal question being asked in our local church should not be "What do I think or want?" The primary collective question being asked in our local church should not be "What do the majority of us think or want?" Such questions can preclude us from discerning and doing God's will for His church.

Rather, our personal and congregational concern should be to prayerfully discern and faithfully do what pleases Jesus Christ, our Savior and Lord. Let us prayerfully acknowledge that Jesus is the supreme head of our local congregation. If we know and agree that we are His body and His church, then our deepest personal and shared longing will be to honor Him in who we are and in all we do.

We can all admit that our sin nature easily leads us to focus on "me, me, me"; that is, we focus on what we think or want. Selfish motivations too easily remain in our hearts and become evident in our local churches. The New Testament letters that were addressed to local churches give ample evidence of this.

For example, in 1 Corinthians, several instances are seen of church members being more focused on pleasing themselves than on discerning and doing what would honor Jesus. Because of this, divisions arose in that early church as described, for example, in 1 Corinthians 1:10-17 and again in 1 Corinthians 3.

Although pride and boasting were rampant in the Corinthian church, the congregation had failed to address it. Neither had they confronted egregious sexual sin that was present in their congregation. The reason for this was made clear in 1 Corinthians 5. Desiring to please themselves and to not dissatisfy or upset any of their members had become for them a higher goal than honoring Jesus Christ.

In 1 Corinthians 10, Paul gave another example of the church having become more focused on satisfying themselves than on pleasing Jesus. It concerned their differences of opinion about whether Christians should eat meat that was previously offered to an idol. Many or most Jewish Christians were saying, "Absolutely not," for they considered this to be sin. Some gentile Christians who were accustomed to eating such meat saw this as no problem at all, so they freely bought and ate such meat without regard for their brothers and sisters in Christ who were very troubled by it.

The Christians who were buying and eating meat offered to idols were unconcerned that their choices could tempt their brothers or sisters to sin. It would be sin for them to acquiesce, as it is when we do anything that we believe dishonors the Lord. The point Paul was addressing was not so much whether it was okay to eat such meat, but that it is not okay for the Lord's Church to focus only on satisfying themselves. We are to be concerned with honoring Jesus by having genuine concern for one another.

Paul summarized his point this way: *So whether you eat or drink, or whatever you do, do it all for the glory of God. Don't give offense to Jews or Gentiles or the church of God. I, too, try to please everyone in everything I do. I don't just do what is best for me; I do what is best for others so that many may be saved. And you should imitate me, just as I imitate Christ* (1 Corinthians 10:31-11:1).

When church members think that the church should be satisfying them whenever they inevitably find themselves unsatisfied about something, the Enemy can and will use such distorted notions to tempt and urge them to leave, and some will leave. However, local churches do not exist to satisfy us.

Our local churches are to please Jesus and do His will. Each member of the local church is to prayerfully ensure that their focus is not on satisfying themselves, but on pleasing Jesus. Each local church is to regularly reinforce its covenant with one another and with the Lord Jesus, that they do indeed belong to Him. The local church of which we are part exists for His honor, glory, and pleasure. So let our prayerful aim be to love Jesus most and to love one another as He has loved us.

For personal reflection: What are some of the implications for you personally that the focus of your own life, and the focus of the church, is not to be on satisfying yourself, but on glorifying God?

For local church leaders' discussion: What are some implications for your local church that, biblically speaking, your aim is not to be on satisfying yourselves or pleasing others? How does this affect how decisions are made among you as church leaders and within the congregation?

5. The Church is not hierarchical nor authoritarian. In the Judaism of Jesus's day, religious authority was both hierarchical and authoritarian. "Hierarchical" refers to something arranged according to levels of importance or rank. It describes organizations in which elements are systematically organized in a way so that some are above, below, or at the same level as others.

Secular governments and militaries are by nature hierarchical systems, and corporations and businesses typically are too. In hierarchical systems, those who are higher in the hierarchy are afforded much more esteem and privilege, so are considered to be more important than those who are lower in the hierarchy.

The term "authoritarian" refers to presumptions and expectations of control. This can include the demands or presumptions of blind submission to those who are in positions of authority. Authoritarian people tell others what to do, and they do so in an autocratic or arrogant manner.

The term "authoritarian" implies that the person or persons in charge are expecting or demanding obedience. They do not want or allow freedom to think or act otherwise. Too many people experience what it means to live in an authoritarian system. Do we presume that successful organizations will always be led in this manner?

Jesus's disciples presumed that the kingdom Jesus was establishing would be hierarchical and authoritarian. His disciples, therefore, secretly longed to be personally elevated to positions of higher or highest esteem. With this in mind, James and John, the two sons of Zebedee, boldly approached Jesus to request such positions. They dreamed of being nearer the top of the hierarchical ladder, holding higher authority and obtaining the benefits that would surely come with such positions.

Because Jesus desired something very different for His disciples then and for His Church now, He used their request as an opportunity to teach them and us. Jesus taught that in His Church, those who will serve will be the greatest of all.

> *"Then James and John, the sons of Zebedee, came over and spoke to Him. "Teacher," they said, "we want you to do us a favor."*
>
> *"What is your request?" Jesus asked.*
>
> *They replied, "When you sit on your glorious throne, we want to sit in places of honor next to you, one on your right and the other on your left."*
>
> *But Jesus said to them, "You don't know what you are asking! Are you able to drink from the bitter cup of suffering I am about to drink? Are you able to be baptized with the baptism of suffering I must be baptized with?"*
>
> *"Oh yes," they replied, "we are able!"*
>
> *Then Jesus told them, "You will indeed drink from my bitter cup and be baptized with my baptism of suffering. But I have no right to say who will sit on my right or my left. God has prepared those places for the ones he has chosen."*
>
> *When the ten other disciples heard what James and John had asked, they were indignant. So Jesus called them together and said, "You know that the rulers in this world lord it over their people, and officials flaunt their authority over those under them. But among you it will be different. Whoever wants to be a leader among you must be your servant, and whoever wants to be first among you must be the slave of everyone else. For even the Son of Man came not to be served but to serve others and to give his life as a ransom for many."* (Mark 10:35-45)

Jesus was telling His disciples, including us, that this aim is wrong. The church is neither hierarchical nor authoritarian. Our aims in the church are not to be climbing the hierarchy of power to gain more and more esteem and influence. Jesus's aim for us is to become more and more like Him. Jesus testified that He *came not to be served but to serve others and to give his life as a ransom for many.*

Referencing the religious leaders of that day, Jesus taught that He wants His disciples and His Church to live differently. Jesus taught that He wants us to lead His church with much humility, not drawing attention to ourselves, but serving like Jesus did. Jesus said to His disciples, including to us and our churches:

> *They crush people with unbearable religious demands and never lift a finger to ease the burden. Everything they do is for show. On their arms they wear extra wide prayer boxes with Scripture verses inside, and they wear robes with extra long tassels. And they love to sit at the head table at banquets and in the seats of honor in the synagogues. They love to receive respectful greetings as they walk in the marketplaces, and to be called "Rabbi."*

> *Don't let anyone call you "Rabbi," for you have only one teacher, and all of you are equal as brothers and sisters. And don't address anyone here on earth as "Father," for only God in heaven is your Father. And don't let anyone call you "Teacher," for you have only one teacher, the Messiah. The greatest among you must be a servant. But those who exalt themselves will be humbled, and those who humble themselves will be exalted."* (Matthew 23:4-12)

Jesus was teaching this new paradigm of organizational leadership. He made it very clear that He did not and does not want His disciples and leaders of His churches to be as worldly leaders, motivated by power or external adulation.

Jesus desires His churches to be led by people who have and demonstrate servant hearts, like Jesus. He made a similar point after instituting

Holy Communion. This was to be and remains an ongoing reminder of His sacrificial death and of His giving of His body and blood for His beloved Church.

But amazingly and sadly, the disciples were arguing with one another again about their self-interests and relative self-importance. Because they all sensed that Messiah Jesus would soon be crowned king, they were dreaming and arguing about who among them would hold positions of highest esteem in the hierarchy of Christ's kingdom, to thus exert more authority and influence.

But they had it all wrong. Our local churches today also must be careful that we do not get this wrong. In biblical local churches, our loving service is to be of higher value than the perceived prestige of higher authority.

> *Then they began to argue among themselves about who would be the greatest among them. Jesus told them, "In this world the kings and great men lord it over their people, yet they are called 'friends of the people.' But among you it will be different. Those who are the greatest among you should take the lowest rank, and the leader should be like a servant. Who is more important, the one who sits at the table or the one who serves? The one who sits at the table, of course. But not here! For I am among you as one who serves."*
> (Luke 22:24-27)

In our local churches and for all members of the churches, our Lord wants our personal aim to be to love, serving like Jesus. For this to be so, we must see that the Church is neither hierarchical nor authoritarian. Humble service must be a higher aim for us than hierarchical or positional authority.

For personal reflection: How has the Lord's elevation of those who serve affected you personally?

For local church leaders' discussion: What are some implications for your local church that, biblically speaking, you are neither hierarchical nor authoritarian? How does this affect the way you lead His Church?

6. The church is not democratic. Contrary to too-common notions about local church governance, our Lord never intended for His Church to function democratically. What exactly is democratic government?

Abraham Lincoln, the sixteenth president of the United States, presided over a deeply divided nation through the horror and chaos of the Civil War. In his Gettysburg Address on November 19, 1863, as the burial ground was being consecrated for the soldiers who had died on the battlefield there, he rightly defined the essence of democratic government. He called it a "government of the people, by the people, for the people."

About a year and a half after delivering that speech, President Lincoln was assassinated, his death illustrating the hatred and division of humanity, even in the frailty of democracies. Democratic governance means that decisions are entrusted to the people who choose their own leaders, and majority vote rules the day.

There are many forms of secular government, all of which are at some level of the people, by the people, and for the people. The primary differences in secular governance seem to be how many of the people's interests are represented.

As a lifelong citizen of the USA, I understand that I was blessed to live in a nation whose government, as imperfect as it is, is to some degree democratic, as it has afforded so many freedoms that I have enjoyed. The collective hope is that the wisdom of the majority may steer the government in the right way. But it doesn't always work that way. Sometimes the majority can get it wrong.

So when it comes to biblical governance, is democracy the right way for the church to go? Is God's will intended to be discerned through majority vote? The perception that biblical church governance is to be democratic is ultimately a false notion. It is a contrived image having no biblical basis. In actuality, the church of Jesus Christ is theocratic, not democratic.

Simply put, a government of the people and by the people is not led by God. Do you want a biblical example? Remember how the people of Israel insisted that they wanted a government like other people had? The Lord repeatedly told them that they did not need a king like other nations had because they had God. God had led them thus far by faith, and they could fully trust God to lead them now. But they insisted, didn't they? The people of Israel wanted government their way, and we know over time that their experiment did not go well.

The Bible says that at the end of the age, Jesus Christ, who is King of kings and Lord of lords, is coming to establish His government. It will have no semblance of democracy. Isaiah 9:6 says, *The government will rest on his shoulders.* That means that the whole government will rest on Jesus. What Jesus says goes. Nothing will be ruled by committee, majority vote, or strong-armed convincing by key leaders. Jesus will reign everywhere.

Isaac Watts (1674-1748) was an English Congregational minister, theologian, and hymnwriter, having written about 750 hymns, including "When I Survey the Wondrous Cross," "Am I a Soldier of the Cross?," "Joy to the World," and "O God, Our Help in Ages Past." One of Isaac Watts's hymns, "Jesus Shall Reign Where're the Sun," beautifully captures the vision of that day when Jesus will reign throughout the world. This hymn is considered by many to be the first great missionary hymn, as it was written at a time when the church was doing little missionary work. But as the Holy Spirit began to move, the message of the gospel went out.

Watts envisioned a day when Jesus would reign throughout the entire world – wherever the sun shines, from shore to shore. His original verses envisioned a time when all people – princes, savage tribes, and people of all languages, even infants – would praise Jesus's name.

This dream is becoming reality, for as the sun makes its journey around the world, Christians in every time zone awaken to praise, love, and serve the Lord Jesus Christ. We are blessed to be Christ's Church under His rule and reign.

I am by no means suggesting it is wrong for the people of God to listen to one another and to prayerfully share their perspectives on various matters. I am also not suggesting it is wrong for a congregation to vote about important matters such as who should become our pastors or leaders, what our faith budget should be for the coming year, or what should be done regarding the Lord's property? But we must know that the church is not a democracy. It is a theocracy. Knowing this, whether we are church leaders making decisions or church congregations making decisions, our aim and focus must shift from asking and determining, "What do I want?" or "What do the majority of the people want?" Our prayerful aim must always be to discern, "What would Jesus have us do?"

This latter question is the one we all must be asking in His Church because there is only one head, one King and Lord, and it is not any of us, nor is it all of us. It is Jesus Christ. Therefore, much prayer is required if our hearts are to beat with Jesus's heart and our thoughts are to align with His thoughts so that His will becomes ours.

If it is a particularly important, troubling, difficult, or divisive issue that we are considering, fasting should be encouraged. But if we are truly desiring the Lord's will above our own, the prayers we pray will be like this: "Dear Father in heaven, in Jesus's name we pray, let Your kingdom come and Your will be done. Let Your will become my will. Bring us to unity in the Holy Spirit so that we may discern and do Your will together. You are my King and Lord, and You are head of this church. We are and will forever be wholly Yours. Amen."

Whether your local church's structure is essentially episcopal, presbyterian, congregational, or another form of governance, if your true aim is to be biblical in church life together, you must let go of any notion that church governance means determining and doing whatever the majority wants. Though this framework may apply in secular government, it does not apply in biblical churches.

The Church of Jesus Christ is not governed democratically because He is our supreme Lord, King, and Head. The good news for local churches is that if and when we are seeking the mind of Jesus Christ together, He reveals it to us. This assurance was given by Jesus through the apostle Paul to the local church in Corinth, and it applies now to all local churches. *Who can know the LORD's thoughts? Who knows enough to teach him? But we understand these things, for we have the mind of Christ* (1 Corinthians 2:16).

Because of this, biblical local churches and leaders will therefore accept the reality that Jesus's desire for His Church will not always align with our personal preferences or comfort zone or what our earthly wisdom suggests would be best. For example, who of us is naturally inclined toward self-denial or taking up our cross daily to follow Him (Matthew 16:24)?

For all followers of Jesus Christ, and so in every local church, it must be okay with us if or when our Lord's will differs from what we would personally choose. As we have confessed, Jesus Christ is Lord, and we are not. In our local churches, our aim, therefore, is to emulate

Jesus by considering others in our church family as so precious to us that we willingly sacrifice ourselves, laying aside personal comfort or preferences for their sakes.

Paul put it this way in a letter addressed to the local church in Philippi: *Don't be selfish; don't try to impress others. Be humble, thinking of others as better than yourselves. Don't look out only for your own interests, but take an interest in others, too. You must have the same attitude that Christ Jesus had* (Philippians 2:3-5).

Let our shared desire be to show Jesus in how we love, forgive, and seek God's best for each other and for His Church. This means that in our local churches, our focus will not be on having our own way or trying to convince others to join our side. Rather, let our personal desires and shared goals be to honor Jesus Christ by discerning and doing His will. Because there are diverse opinions among us, our process of discernment has to go beyond sharing personal opinions or trying to convince others to agree with us. Our approach must begin and end with loving God most and loving one another.

Times of prayer must prevail also, perhaps with times of fasting. As we pray, we are to lay aside all personal agendas and opinions, humbly asking and desiring the Lord to make His way clear, and believing that He will. Our shared commitment must be to know our Lord's will, and then to honor Him by doing His will.

During my years of church leadership, I have learned that when church leaders or congregations face decisions on important matters, our sole task is to discern and do what Jesus desires. For this reason, I would go so far as to urge leaders and members to only weigh in or vote on the matter being considered if they have truly done what I've described here – genuinely, sincerely, and prayerfully seeking the Lord and His will. My reason for this caution is because if anyone does otherwise, they are in real danger of unwittingly advocating a course that is contrary to the Lord's will.

How could we possibly think we can discern the will of the Lord Jesus if we have not prayerfully humbled ourselves before Him? How could we rightly know our Lord's will if we have not humbled ourselves before Him, laying aside personal agendas and judgments to seek His face, listening to Him speak through His Word, and desiring His glory and honor above our own opinions or desires?

Let us discard the deceptive image that suggests local churches can or should be democratic in governance. Let us discard the false notions that we, the members of this congregation, are in charge, that it is our opinions that matter most, and that majority votes are a biblical method for determining the church's course.

In the addendum that I have included on congregationalism at the end of this volume, more insight is shared about how church leaders and members can work together in discerning the mind of Christ for the local church. But the basic principle that underpins biblical church governance for all churches is that the Church of Jesus Christ is theocratic, for He is the head of His body, the Church.

Jesus has given to His church all that we need to discern and do His will. He has given to us the Holy Bible, which is the inspired and infallible written Word of God, through which our Lord speaks to His Church.

The Lord Jesus has also poured out the Holy Spirit upon His Church, gifting and empowering us for His service, opening hearts and minds with spiritual understanding, and equipping us with unity to be His body together. The Holy Spirit enables us to go where the Lord sends us, to say what the Lord gives us to say, and to do what the Lord calls us to do.

Jesus Christ has given us one another in the local church, to be as family, so that none of us is alone. Jesus has blessed each and all of us. He has blessed us immeasurably! Jesus Christ is the head of His body, the Church. It is our personal privilege and shared responsibility to love Him, seek Him, and follow Him as He leads His church.

For personal reflection: What does it mean in your personal life that the church is not democratic, but is theocratic; that He is Lord, and you are not?

For local church leaders' discussion: What are some implications for your local congregation that your church is not democratic, but is theocratic? How does this affect the way you lead? How does it affect how you model and teach how decisions are to be made biblically, prayerfully discerning the Lord's will?

Chapter 3

Primary Forms of Historic Church Governance

Episcopal, Presbyterian, Congregational

The first chapter in the book of Acts reveals that when the Church started, its structure consisted of twelve apostles in a group of one hundred and twenty faithful followers of Jesus. Acts 2 reports that on the birthday of the Church, after the Holy Spirit had come in power as had been promised by Jesus, three thousand converts were added, and more came to faith in Him every day: *Each day the Lord added to their fellowship those who were being saved* (Acts 2:47).

Acts 4:4 tells us that soon five thousand men were in the church. This was surely in addition to thousands of women and children. Just a few days, weeks, or months later, a sizeable multitude of people were following Jesus Christ in the first local church in the city of Jerusalem.

There were so many followers of Jesus in that church that the apostles could not do all the work that was required to care for them all. Others were soon chosen to assume some of the leadership responsibilities. This marked the beginning of organizing the structures in local church government.

As the church continued to expand, the Holy Spirit gave needed guidance on the administration of the Lord's Church. This included ordaining some offices and designating the necessary qualifications for the leaders. Insights were also given as to how church leaders are called to function.

Three primary offices were referenced in the New Testament and in the writings of early church fathers before the New Testament canon came to be established. In Koine Greek of that time, which was the common language in which the New Testament was written, three original offices of the early church were *episkopos* (bishop/overseer), *presbuteros* (presbyters/elders), and *diakonos* (servants/ deacons). We will consider these three, because in time these led conceptually to three distinct structures of local church governance.

The term "pastor," which means "shepherd," has also been used since the early days of the church, as is seen in the New Testament. It referred to certain ministries of local church leaders. Several of the early church fathers used this term too, but not as a title for a particular church office. To pastor/shepherd was a particular responsibility assigned by the Lord to local church leaders who were overseers or elders.

In Koine Greek, *episkopos* is a compound word. The preposition *epi* (επι) means "on, over, upon, or at," while the noun *skopos* (σκοπός) means "one who watches, looks after, or guards," such as a watchman. This is what shepherds do – they watch over their flocks. In Ezekiel 3:17 and Ezekiel 33:7, the word *skopos* appears in the Septuagint, the Greek translation of the Hebrew Scriptures.

Elsewhere in the New Testament, pastoring/shepherding was assigned to *presbuteros* (elders/presbyters). An example of pastoring/shepherding being assigned to *presbuteros* is found in 1 Peter 5:1-2, which is addressed *to you who are [presbyters] elders in the churches.* There the apostle Peter wrote, *As a fellow [presbyter] elder, I appeal to you: Care for the flock that God has entrusted to you.* The word in this phrase to care for the flock means to shepherd or pastor them.

Also, as seen in Acts 20:28, Paul exhorted the presbyters/elders of the local church in Ephesus, whom he had sent for and so dearly loved. Knowing that he would not see them again on this side of heaven, Paul urged them all to faithfully *feed and shepherd* (pastor) God's flock.

As the pastoral assignment of shepherding God's flock is a biblical calling, the title of pastor is often used to refer to the ones who are given such responsibility in the church. The realization that biblically, "pastor" did not refer to a particular office (as it is often used now), but rather to an assigned responsibility of overseers or elders, illustrates that the church of Jesus Christ has not been uniform in understanding how local church governance should best be formed or what titles should be used.

People equally committed to faith in Jesus Christ and to the authority of the Bible can come to differing conclusions on the best ways for local churches to be structured. Local church governments may take various forms, local churches may use various titles to refer to their leaders, and different congregations can use similar terms but with different meanings.

Despite the variety among structures and terms used in local churches today, there have been three primary forms of church governance in history. Those three are episcopal, presbyterian, and congregational. Each of these has roots in perceptions about one of the early church offices of *episkopos*, *presbuteros*, or *diakonos*.

1. The episcopal form of church administration focuses church authority on a primary executive. The word "episcopal" originates from the Greek word *episkopos*, meaning "bishop." It appears in the Bible as both a noun and a verb, meaning "an overseer" or "the act of overseeing."

   Episcopal church governance is a hierarchical structure in which a bishop or superintendent oversees one or many churches. Local church ministers or priests are assigned to local churches, and there is clear division between clergy and laity.

2. The presbyterian form of church administration focuses local church authority on a group of presbyters as a legislative body. The word "presbytery" comes from the Greek word *presbuteros*. This word appears more often in Scripture than does *episkopos*, and it is typically translated "elders." Fifty-eight of the sixty-seven times this word is used in the New Testament, it is plural, because presbyters function and lead together as a plurality.

   The Koine Greek word *presbuteros*, translated as "elder," refers to an older person. This was a respectful term used for those who had attained a greater age. As words of any language can change meaning over time, this word developed into a title for those who had attained a station of leadership in a family or a society.

   In the context of the church, *presbuteros* was a title for an office of leadership. This word was most often used in the plural because elders were and are to function as a group, discerning the mind of Christ together. This concept of church governance is in contrast to more executive authority exercised by an individual in episcopal governance.

Presbyterian churches apply a legislative form of government. Beyond congregations whose title is presbyterian, all local churches who have a body of elders vested together with authority and responsibility to lead are essentially practicing this form of historic church governance.

3. The congregational form of church administration focuses on the autonomy of each local church under the headship of Jesus. Leaders are chosen and set apart by the members of that local congregation. Love for Jesus and one another is the goal, with shared desire and determination to discern and do His will together. Congregational governance considers authority and responsibility for the local church as belonging to the whole assembly.

The first occasion of selecting local church leaders is seen in Acts 6. In the church of Jerusalem, the apostles gave to *all the believers* (Acts 6:2) – to the entire congregation – the responsibility of choosing some of their number to be *diakonos*, or servants among them. The Bible doesn't say that they voted on the matter, but the congregation clearly agreed, for they chose seven (Acts 6:5-6), whom they presented to the apostles. This is the first recorded instance of congregational governance happening in a local church.

The word "congregation" appears hundreds of times in the Hebrew Old Testament, but not in the Greek New Testament. Several Hebrew synonyms are translated as "congregation" in the Old Testament, but these always refer to a large assembly gathered for a special purpose in a special place. In the New Testament, the one appearance of "congregation" is a translation of the word synagogue: *When the congregation was dismissed, many of the Jews and devout converts to Judaism followed Paul and Barnabas, who talked with them and urged them to continue in the grace of God* (Acts 13:43 NIV). The Greek word *ekklesia*, which means "called-out ones," is a broad equivalent of "congregation," and it is typically translated "church" in the New Testament.

Throughout the history of the Christian Church, the structures of local church governance have taken various forms. The three primary forms that have endured most likely flowed out of differing perspectives concerning the function of church offices mentioned in the New Testament, as well as from the writings of early church fathers. Perceptions about the differing governance models may also have been affected by Christians assessing the relative effectiveness of these structures at various times in being and making disciples of Jesus and growing His church.

Whatever form of governance local churches apply, congregations that aim to be biblical must acknowledge and own that the local church does not belong to us, but belongs to Jesus. His Word will thus be our guide, and His will our shared desire.

Three Timeless Leadership Lessons for Today from Historic Biblical Offices

Recognizing the diversity that is in the Church of Jesus Christ around the world surely includes acknowledging that there are many differences in how local churches are structured. But we know in faith that God is not limited by these differences.

Our Lord offers timeless leadership lessons for our churches. From each of the early church offices of *episkopos*, *presbuteros*, and *diakonos* mentioned in the New Testament, and in letters from early church fathers, we can gain valuable insight for biblical local church leadership today.

Leadership Lesson from *Episkopos*: Senior Leaders Will Oversee the Church

The apostle Paul had this to say to Timothy about the *episkopos*: *The saying is trustworthy: If anyone aspires to the office of overseer* [episkopos], *he desires a noble task. Therefore an overseer must be above reproach* (1 Timothy 3:1-2 ESV). This term was used in reference to several of the early church fathers. Ignatius referred to himself as *episkopos* of Antioch,

Clement was *episkopos* of Rome, and Polycarp was *episkopos* of Smyrna. The term *episkopos*, or a form of it, appears twelve times in the New Testament, but fifty-five times in the early church letters of Ignatius.[2]

These various early references do not seem to imply the system that developed later of bishops overseeing regions of scattered churches. Initially, *episkopos* were local church overseers, entrusted with oversight of a local church.

Some terms used today for this role of *episkopos* include pastor, senior pastor, lead pastor, bishop, or superintendent. No matter what a local church calls the overseer, biblical qualifications that are listed in 1 Timothy 3 include being above reproach, being faithful in marriage, exercising self-control, living wisely, having a good reputation, and being hospitable, gentle, and able to teach. Disqualifying traits include being a heavy drinker, being violent, being a lover of money, being quarrelsome, or having a family that does not respect him.

Responsibilities of *episkopos* are summarized by Paul: *I charge you in the presence of God and of Christ Jesus, who is to judge the living and the dead, and by his appearing and his kingdom: preach the word; be ready in season and out of season; reprove, rebuke, and exhort, with complete patience and teaching* (2 Timothy 4:1-2 ESV).

Ignatius was an early *episkopos* whose testimony still speaks. Before his martyrdom in AD 107, he was overseer of the church of Antioch. Ignatius also penned letters to local churches that were springing up in various cities and towns, for as the good news of Jesus was being proclaimed, the church was spreading.

As Ignatius wrote extensively about local church governance, he seemed to assume that his readers in the new churches sprouting up throughout Asia Minor (modern-day Turkey) were familiar with these leadership offices, which tells us that these offices were already commonly known. This familiarity included the leadership office of *episkopos*, as it was then held by Ignatius in the church of Antioch. Newer and younger congregations and church leaders would have then been especially blessed by receiving the counsel and wisdom of this mature *episkopos*.[3]

---

2 *The Epistles of St. Clement of Rome and St. Ignatius of Antioch,* translated and annotated by James A. Kleist, Ancient Christian Writers, No. 1 (Westminster, MD: Newman Press, 1978), 143.

3 Kleist, *Epistles,* 143-144

This biblical leadership office is local-church focused, yet also has the Lord's concern for the wider body of Christ. *Episkopos* are assigned by the Lord Jesus to care well for the flock of God to which He has assigned them. This requires every *episkopos* to know the sheep He has entrusted to them to oversee. Biblical churches are therefore local churches that are following Jesus together, being led by loving overseers who are leading the local church in following the Lord.

A Leadership Lesson from *Presbuteros*: Leaders Will Care for God's Flock Together

Because *presbuteros* functioned as a plurality of elders, sharing oversight in a local church, many New Testament scholars believe the term *episkopos* referred to the presiding or senior elder of the local church in a given city. If so, *episkopos* would have been prayerfully chosen from among the faithful presbyters/elders who had demonstrated effectiveness and readiness for this senior oversight responsibility.

The apostle Paul sent a messenger to call the church leadership team of *presbuteros* from Ephesus to come quickly to meet him in the seaport of Miletus, as he was on his way to Jerusalem by sea. The apostle wanted to give them heartfelt and motivating exhortation, which is recorded by Luke in the book of Acts: *But when we landed at Miletus, he sent a message to the elders of the church at Ephesus, asking them to come and meet him* (Acts 20:17).

Upon their arrival, and knowing that he would not be seeing them again on this side of heaven, Paul exhorted this beloved team of *presbuteros*, saying, *Guard yourselves and God's people. Feed and shepherd God's flock—his church, purchased with his own blood—over which the Holy Spirit has appointed you as leaders* (Acts 20:28). He also gave them this warning: *I know that false teachers, like vicious wolves, will come in among you after I leave, not sparing the flock* (Acts 20:29).

Paul was exhorting the *presbuteros* team to care for the flock of God together. In the early years of the Church, as local churches were being established, Paul tasked Titus to appoint elders in every city (Titus 1:5). Then and now, every local church requires shared leadership. We can presume that early on, many local churches were not yet large enough to have raised a team of elders. This is still true today where new churches are being planted, but team leadership is always to be a biblical goal.

The apostle Paul gave Titus a list of the necessary qualifications for serving as a local church elder. Titus would have applied this guidance, and biblical churches will do so now. The apostle instructed:

> I left you on the island of Crete so you could complete our work there and appoint elders in each town as I instructed you. An elder must live a blameless life. He must be faithful to his wife, and his children must be believers who don't have a reputation for being wild or rebellious. A church leader is a manager of God's household, so he must live a blameless life. He must not be arrogant or quick-tempered; he must not be a heavy drinker, violent, or dishonest with money.
>
> Rather, he must enjoy having guests in his home, and he must love what is good. He must live wisely and be just. He must live a devout and disciplined life. He must have a strong belief in the trustworthy message he was taught; then he will be able to encourage others with wholesome teaching and show those who oppose it where they are wrong. (Titus 1:5-9)

In this instructive passage, Paul used the term *presbuteros* (presbyter/elder) in verses 5 and 6, but in verse 7 he switched to the term *episkopos* (bishop/overseer). Some have suggested that Paul was using these terms interchangeably, but if that were so it would not explain why he more commonly used the term *presbuteros*.

It seems more likely that because presbyters were plural and were to lead as a team, there would have been many, especially in larger congregations. But *episkopos*, or bishops/overseers, were fewer, and there may have typically been only one, so these two terms were not wholly interchangeable. But because *episkopos* were also *presbuteros*, much of the guidance given by the apostle applied to both of these offices.

Biblical tasks of local church elders include serving, guiding, and guarding the church together. Several key leaders of the early church, who are referred to as church fathers, mentioned the *presbuteros* in their letters. In AD 96, Clement, who was then *episkopos* of Rome, wrote to the church of Corinth, urging them to "Submit to the *presbuteros* and be instructed for repentance with humble hearts."[4]

Another early example of referencing the *presbuteros* is Polycarp, who was then *episkopos* of Smyrna. Polycarp had been a disciple of the apostle John, and in AD 155 he was martyred because of his faith in Jesus Christ and his refusal to renounce Christ. In his letter to the local church at Philippi, Polycarp expressed personal greetings from himself and from the *presbuteros* who were with him.[5]

The biblical leadership role of *presbuteros* still speaks to local churches. Local congregations must not consider their pastors to be solely responsible for the ministry of the church. Neither should local congregations appoint church leaders but then impede or refuse to follow their leadership.

The biblical model of *presbuteros* requires selecting a leadership team comprised of people meeting the biblical qualifications, who then join with the pastor or overseer by laying aside personal agendas and seeking the mind of Christ together. Leaders who are seeking and following the Lord Jesus like this are enabled to lead the congregation in following Him too. Local church members must allow the leaders to lead, as Jesus Christ is leading them.

Local churches can choose to apply this biblical principle in different ways. Some elect presbyters/elders. Others may identify different structures or terms that might include a church council, vestry, diaconate, governing board, or another name. But basic ingredients of a biblical model for local church governance always includes developing and having a team of spiritually mature servant leaders who seek the mind of Jesus Christ together, caring well for His Church, and leading as Christ leads them.

---

4   *Clement of Rome and the Didache*, "Letter to the Corinthians," translated and commentary by Kenneth J. Howell, Early Christian Fathers Series (Zanesville, OH, CHResources, 2012) 56

5   *Polycarp's Letter to the Philippians & His Martyrdom*, narrated by Lamar Peugh (GodSounds Inc., 2016), section 1.

Leadership Lesson from Diakonos: Servant Leaders Will Serve Like Jesus

A third leadership title that is used in the New Testament and in the early Church is *diakonos* (deacons). This Koine Greek word means "servant." In a local church, it refers to individuals designated by the congregation as servant leaders.

Diakonos were spiritually mature and qualified people (1 Timothy 3:8-13; Romans 16:1) who modeled servant hearts like Jesus Christ did (John 13:12-17). Deacons were chosen by the congregation from among members of that local church (Acts 6:1-7). They were responsible together for addressing that local church's needs and charitable outreach.

The apostle Paul mentions deacons in the opening of his letter to the local church in Philippi: *To all the saints in Christ Jesus who are at Philippi, with the overseers and deacons* (Philippians 1:1 ESV). Paul instructed Timothy about the necessary qualifications of deacons, concluding, *Those who do well as deacons will be rewarded with respect from others and will have increased confidence in their faith in Christ Jesus* (1 Timothy 3:13).

The ministry of local church deacons was also mentioned in writings of various early church leaders. Around AD 100, in his letter to the local church in Ephesus, Ignatius of Antioch said that it would be impossible to have the church without deacons or other ministers who "continue the ministry of Jesus Christ."[6]

Local churches require servant leaders who can ensure that no one among them is neglected or feeling unloved. Toward this end, local churches can choose to structure their servant leadership in different ways. Some may refer to chosen servant leaders as deacons, and some will use another name.

But biblically, all local churches under the headship of Jesus Christ will need to have caring people who reflect Jesus's servant heart in caring for the congregation and leading the members in doing the same. So the leadership lesson from *diakonos* is that servant leaders with servant hearts will serve like Jesus.

To review, in the biblical offices of *episkopos*, *presbuteros*, and *diakonos*, there are lessons to be learned and still applied in biblical local churches. Those lessons include:

---

6   Paul Trabilico, *The Early Christians in Ephesus from Paul to Ignatius* (Grand Rapids: William B. Eerdmans, 2007), 639.

- Senior leaders will oversee Christ's church.

- Leaders will care for God's flock together.

- Servant leaders will serve like Jesus.

For personal reflection: What are applications for you personally of the lessons learned from the historic biblical offices of *episkopos, presbuteros,* and *diakonos*?

For local church leaders' discussion: How are the principles learned in these historic biblical offices currently applied in structures and ministries of your local church? What changes could the Lord be calling you to prayerfully make?

Chapter 4

Levels of Authority and Responsibility in Biblical Local Churches

Headship, Leadership, Membership

Three levels of authority and responsibility as defined in God's Word for all local churches are headship, leadership, and membership. These three apply no matter how a local church is structured. Churches aiming to be biblical in life and ministry will prayerfully apply these three.

Biblical Principles on Headship in Local Churches

This is the foundation of the Church, and this is what Jesus meant when He taught His followers to build their lives upon the solid rock. In Matthew 7:24-27, Jesus was teaching about the kingdom of heaven. Because He is the ruler of this kingdom, those who are wise are going to hear Jesus's teachings and obey them. In doing so, they are building upon a foundation of solid rock and so will withstand any storm in life.

Those who are foolish may hear what Jesus has said, but they do not obey. In doing so, they are building upon a foundation of sand. Even if that house looks beautiful on sunny days, it will surely collapse when the inevitable storms come. This message applies to individuals and also to local churches.

The foundation upon which biblical local churches must be built is the person of Jesus Christ. And so the first level of authority in all biblical local churches is the headship of Jesus Christ! If ever a local church is not believing, understanding, and living this absolute truth together, that group of people is building upon sand and is missing what it means to be a biblical congregation.

In local churches that are biblical in life and practice, the head of the church truly is Jesus Christ. He is in the position of highest authority, and church leaders and members alike are living accordingly. We want, invite, and allow Jesus to lead us in all things.

The highest and ultimate authority in the global church and in every local church belongs to Jesus Christ. Just before He ascended into heaven, Jesus said, *I have been given all authority in heaven and on earth* (Matthew 28:18). He meant what He said. All authority means just that. Jesus has it all. The head of the Church and of every local church is the Son of God, the Lord Jesus Christ.

Do we understand this? When we understand and accept this truth, the way that we personally live as disciples of Jesus Christ, and the way that we function as local churches, will be markedly different.

What did Peter confess when Jesus asked, *Who do you say I am?* (Matthew 16:15). Peter declared to the Lord of all what we are blessed and called to declare now: *You are the Messiah, the Son of the Living God* (Matthew 16:16).

What was Jesus's reply? Jesus said, *Upon this rock I will build my church, and all the powers of hell will not conquer it* (Matthew 16:18).

Whose Church did Jesus say it was? He said, *I will build my church.* The Church that Jesus is building is His. Local church leaders, we are incapable of building or leading the church on our own because it isn't ours. It is His. Because Jesus calls it *my church*, all who would lead it, and all who are part of it, are to let go of personal ownership and preferences in order to focus their hearts on discerning and doing the will of the one who is the foundation of our very being and the head of the Church, even the Lord Jesus Christ.

Rev. Everett Leslie "Terry" Fullam was a priest, biblical scholar, and teacher who gained prominence in the Episcopal Church in the United States, and in the Anglican, Roman Catholic, and evangelical communities worldwide for his renewal ministries from 1972 to 1998. I first heard of Terry Fullam when I was attending Barrington College in Rhode Island, where he had been a professor of theology. Years later while I was serving as a local church pastor in Rhode Island, I read Bob Slosser's book *Miracle in Darien*, which described Fullam's renewal ministry at Saint Paul's Church in Darien, Connecticut. The book was acknowledged then as a significant text on church renewal, and I found it very encouraging.

Terry Fullam and St. Paul's Episcopal Church, which was of course episcopal in their governance, began hosting conferences for leadership teams from local churches of various denominations and structures. I and several other leaders of the congregational church that I then served attended one of these conferences.

One key lesson I took away from that conference that powerfully impacted my understanding of biblical local church leadership concerned implications of this truth that Jesus Christ is head of the church. In episcopal governance, the local church leadership team is generally referred to as a vestry. I remember Terry Fullam's story about his first meeting with the vestry of St. Paul's Episcopal Church, which happened on the second day of his job as rector (senior pastor). He described opening his Bible in that first meeting and reading various portions of Paul's letters on this theme of Jesus as head of the Church. Included among his readings was this passage addressed to the church in Ephesus:

> *I also pray that you will understand the incredible greatness of God's power for us who believe him. This is the same mighty power that raised Christ from the dead and seated him in the place of honor at God's right hand in the heavenly realms. Now he is far above any ruler or authority or power or leader or anything else—not only in this world but also in the world to come. God has put all things under the authority of Christ and has made him head over all things for the benefit of the church. And the church is his body; it is made full and complete by Christ, who fills all things everywhere with himself.* (Ephesians 1:19-23)

Other referenced passages that day included Romans 12, 1 Corinthians 12, and Colossians 1. Terry Fullam said that after reading these scriptures that day, he looked around at the members of the gathered vestry and asked, "What are some implications of this, that Jesus Christ is head of His body, the church – even of St. Paul's Church?"

After saying this, he remained silent, waiting until someone answered. After several moments, one vestry member looked at his newly arrived rector and firmly said, "If Jesus is head of this church, then you are not!" Fullam agreed. And so began the Holy Spirit teaching that church the implications of this important truth.

Three Implications of the Headship of Jesus in the Local Church

1. A first implication of the headship of Jesus in the local church is that since Jesus is the head of His church, I am not, and we are not! The pastor is not the head of the church, nor are church leaders. Members are not in charge either. Jesus Christ is the head of His church.

2. A second implication of the headship of Jesus in the local church is that since Jesus is the head, He surely has a plan for us. What would then be an obvious conclusion that local church leaders and members should make?

   Since Jesus, who is the head of His Church including this local church, surely has a plan for us, our highest priority and ultimate responsibility must be to discern His plan and do it. We can know in faith that of course Jesus will make a way for us to fulfill His plan.

   Terry Fullam's biblical reminder includes the fact that Jesus wants us to see this local church as He sees it. We are much more than an organized social group. We are the living body of Christ, and Jesus is our head.

3. A third implication of the headship of Jesus in the local church is that since Jesus is the head of His Church, He desires to lead us together in unity. This implication is clear. Surely God would not divide His body, nor would He give conflicting messages about the ways He would have us go. He will guide rightly those who allow Him to, remembering what He taught about building life and His church upon the solid rock. God says, *I will guide you along the best pathway for your life. I will advise you and watch*

over you. Do not be like a senseless horse or mule that needs a bit and bridle to keep it under control (Psalm 32:8-9).

In several letters to local churches, Paul focused on our calling to unity in Christ Jesus. One example was near the beginning of his first letter to the church in Corinth: *I appeal to you, dear brothers and sisters, by the authority of our Lord Jesus Christ, to live in harmony with each other. Let there be no divisions in the church. Rather, be of one mind, united in thought and purpose* (1 Corinthians 1:10).

This exhortation still speaks to local churches today under the headship of Christ. Below are a few other scriptures on this theme of unity in local church life:

Make me truly happy by agreeing wholeheartedly with each other, loving one another, and working together with one mind and purpose. (Philippians 2:2)

Then the apostles and elders together with the whole church in Jerusalem chose delegates, and they sent them to Antioch of Syria with Paul and Barnabas to report on this decision. . . . So we decided, having come to complete agreement, to send you official representatives, along with our beloved Barnabas and Paul. . . . For it seemed good to the Holy Spirit and to us to lay no greater burden on you than these few requirements. (Acts 15:22, 25, 28)

So a first and highest level of authority in all biblical local churches is the headship of Jesus!

For personal reflection: What are some implications for you personally in regard to the headship of Jesus Christ in your own life and of your local church?

For local church leaders' discussion: What are implications for you as church leaders, and for your congregation, that Jesus Christ is the head of your local church? Discuss how each of these is being modeled, taught, and applied in your church:

- Since Jesus is the head of His church, I am not, and we are not!

- Since Jesus is the head of His church, He surely has a plan for us!

- Since Jesus is the head of His church, He desires to lead us together in unity.

We are looking at three levels of authority and responsibility defined in God's Word that are for all local churches. The first is headship. The second is leadership.

Leadership in Biblical Local Churches

Biblical local churches will have leaders who are called of God to lead and who are recognized and affirmed as leaders by members of the congregation. No one can rightly lead a local church under the headship of Jesus unless He has called them and therefore equips them for the task.

As local church leaders follow Jesus Christ, members who also follow Jesus will gladly follow those whom God has called to lead. Church leaders, like our Good Shepherd, can only guide those who will hear and follow His voice.

Jesus said that those whom He calls will hear and recognize His voice and will follow Him. Jesus leads, and we follow His lead. This is where all church leadership begins. As sheep follow their shepherd's familiar voice, Christians follow the leaders appointed by Jesus Christ who faithfully follow Him. *He calls his own sheep by name and leads them out. After he has gathered his own flock, he walks ahead of them, and they follow him because they know his voice. They won't follow a stranger; they will run from him because they don't know his voice* (John 10:3-5).

Local churches can be structured in varied ways, using diverse titles for leaders. But in all biblical local churches, Jesus raises up leaders to follow Him and lead the congregation to do the same. With this in mind, we will consider three principles that apply to all local church leaders under Jesus's headship.

Three Biblical Principles for Local Church Leadership under Jesus's Headship

1. Biblical local church leaders personally yield to Jesus Christ. The apostle Paul modeled this for us when urging members of the local church in Corinth to imitate him. He started the letter by urging them to *imitate me, just as I imitate Christ* (1 Corinthians 11:1). This word, *imitate*, appears five other times in the New Testament – in 1 Corinthians 4:16, Ephesians 5:1, 1 Thessalonians 1:6, 1 Thessalonians 2:14, and Hebrews 6:12.

Jesus desires all church leaders to live lives yielded to Him, thus setting an example for others to see, imitate, and follow. This brings all church leaders to this important personal question: Who is the Lord of my life?

"As a student at Fuller Theological Seminary, studying late one night for a Greek exam, Bill Bright receive[d] a unique impression from God to invest his life in helping reach the entire world, starting with college students. A professor friend suggest[ed] 'Campus Crusade for Christ' as the name of the new ministry. In the fall, Bill and his wife, Vonette, start[ed] Campus Crusade (now known as Cru in the U.S.) at UCLA with the backing of a 24-hour prayer chain." This international Christian outreach ministry is now located in 191 nations.[7]

Bill Bright encouraged Christians to ask spiritual questions when the Lord gave them an opportunity in personal conversations. In the United States, where his ministry started, he met many college students who thought they were Christians either because they had some church connection in the past or because they were not following any other religion. But he found that many of these people had little or no concept of what it meant to love and follow Jesus. Bill Bright would often take a piece of paper and draw a heart with a throne in the center. He would say that this was a picture of their heart, and the question for them was, "Who sits on the throne? Is it you or Jesus?"

Biblical church leaders are people who are living with Jesus on the throne of their heart. By words and deeds, they show what it means to be personally yielded to Jesus Christ. In biblical local churches, leadership teams will be comprised of people who believe, say, live, and show that Jesus Christ is Lord.

---

7   https://www.cru.org/us/en/about.html#history.

The shared focus among church leadership teams is prayerfully seeking, discerning and doing the Lord's will through and for His church. Being ourselves under the authority of Jesus enables us to lead His church to yield to Him too.

This requirement was evident in the first account of church leaders being chosen, as described in Acts 6. The apostles had directed the church in Jerusalem to select deacons from among themselves. The Bible says they chose seven who were *full of the Spirit and wisdom* (Acts 6:3).

Stephen was among those seven chosen leaders, for he was known to be *a man full of faith and of the Holy Spirit* (Acts 6:5). The next chapter of Acts shows the depth of Stephen's devotion to Jesus, for he boldly testified of his faith in Christ before a hostile crowd, and in so doing he gave his life as the first recorded Christian martyr. Stephen embodied this first biblical principle for local church leadership of being personally yielded to Jesus Christ.

2. Biblical local church leaders oversee Christ's church as under-shepherds. Jacob watched over the sheep that belonged to his father-in-law, Laban. Moses watched over the sheep that belonged to his father-in-law, Jethro. David watched over the sheep that belonged to his father, Jesse. In the same way, we who are called to lead Christ's church watch over Jesus's flock as His under-shepherds. Paul's clearest words in the New Testament on this theme were addressed to the elders of the church in Ephesus. He urged them: *Guard yourselves and God's people. Feed and shepherd God's flock—his church, purchased with his own blood—over which the Holy Spirit has appointed you as leaders* (Acts 20:28).

Biblical church leaders who realize this will often pause to consider that the local church is the flock for whom Christ died. We realize in all humility that Jesus Christ, who is the Good Shepherd and head of His body, the church, has entrusted their care to us as His under-shepherds. We watch over the Lord's flock for Him.

3. Biblical local church leaders are to serve like Jesus, giving of themselves in His name. We will continually recall Jesus's sacrifice for us on the cross and His example of servanthood as portrayed in John 13. Our Lord Jesus humbled Himself as a servant, washing all of His disciples' dirty feet. Upon concluding, Jesus addressed these who were to become the initial leaders of His church and exemplars for future generations. He said, *Since I, your Lord and Teacher, have washed your feet, you ought to wash each other's feet. I have given you an example to follow. Do as I have done to you* (John 13:14-15).

Biblical local church leaders who are serving like Jesus will prioritize others' needs over their own. This will mean using time, talents, gifts, and strength to assist others. It will include being open to interruptions and prepared for challenges. Biblical church leaders serve with consideration, being open to surprising outcomes.

In review, we have seen these biblical principles for all local church leaders under the headship of Jesus:

- Local church leaders personally yield to Jesus Christ.

- Local church leaders oversee Christ's church as His under-shepherds.

- Local church leaders serve like Jesus, giving of themselves in His name.

For personal reflection: What are some implications for you personally and for your local church leaders of these biblical requirements of leadership under the headship of Christ?

For local church leaders' discussion: What are some implications of each of these biblical requirements for you personally, as church leaders together, and for your local church?

Biblical Principles on Membership in Local Churches

We are examining three levels of biblical authority and responsibility in all local churches, and thus far we have considered biblical principles on the headship of Jesus Christ, and on local church leadership under Christ's headship. The third level of authority in biblical local churches is membership.

Biblical churches are comprised of members who are trusting in Jesus Christ as Savior and have thus entered a covenant relationship with Christ and so with one another in Christ. We will now explore:

Six Biblical Principles for All Church Members
to Live Under Jesus's Headship

A. Church members aim to love like Jesus

Knowing the Lord Jesus, who gave His life for us, church members have believed and receive God's great love for us. Our new life in Christ has brought us into a personal relationship with God. This has led us to gladly covenant to love the Lord our God and to love one another and all those whom God calls us to love. Yes, we will fall short of always loving like Jesus. But with hearts of love for our loving Lord, this will be our shared aim.

We remember Jesus's answer when someone asked Him one day, *Of all the commandments, which is the most important?* (Mark 12:28). In reply, Jesus quoted two passages of Scripture. First, Jesus quoted Deuteronomy 6:4-5. He said, *The LORD our God is the one and only LORD. And you must love the LORD your God with all your heart, all your soul, all your mind, and all your strength* (Mark 12:29-30). Then, quoting Leviticus 19:18, He said, *The second is equally important: "Love your neighbor as yourself." No other commandment is greater than these* (Mark 12:31).

As the time was fast approaching when Jesus would lay down His life for us, He gave a powerful mandate for all who would love and follow Him. He said, *I am giving you a new commandment: Love each other. Just as I have loved you, you should love each other. Your love for one another will prove to the world that you are my disciples* (John 13:34-35).

This is an extremely high calling for us, isn't it? Because it is the highest biblical principle for church members to live together under Jesus's headship, let's flesh out what it looks like for local church members to love one another. How can we love one another like Jesus has loved us? Following are seven ways.

Seven Ways Local Church Members Can
Be Loving to One Another

1. Gather with one another. Whenever we gather together, we do so in the name and in the love of Jesus Christ our Lord. When Christians meet together, in large groups or small, Christ is present among us, as

He promised to be when He said, *Where two or three gather together as my followers, I am there among them* (Matthew 18:20).

Whenever we gather together, the Holy Spirit is among us and in us and wants us all to be receptive to His leading and available for whatever He might have us receive or give. To the local church in Corinth, Paul instructed, *When you meet together, one will sing, another will teach, another will tell some special revelation God has given, one will speak in tongues, and another will interpret what is said. But everything that is done must strengthen all of you* (1 Corinthians 14:26).

Doing this allows divine-appointment opportunities to give and receive Christ's love, and so to be loving one another. It might be in a corporate worship gathering or in a small-group meeting for prayer and study. It might be when visiting friends of the church who can no longer get out because of age or infirmity, or when meeting a Christian brother or sister to share lunch, prayer, and fellowship. *Let us not neglect our meeting together, as some people do, but encourage one another, especially now that the day of his return is drawing near* (Hebrews 10:25).

2. Live in community with one another. Did you know that there are about one hundred "one another" verses in the Bible? These are specific actions churches are exhorted to do together, including greeting, comforting, serving, showing humility, and showing compassion and kindness to one another. It is simply impossible to live out these "one another" commands with each other without living together in some degree of Christian community.

Christ's church is to *live in harmony with each other* (Romans 12:16). The head of the church calls us to live life-on-life with one another, as in community. In this way we are blessed to experientially love one another.

3. Pray for one another. One of the most loving things we can do for each other is to pray. Love is not shown by merely telling someone, "I will pray for you," but love is shown in actually doing so. Whenever it is possible for us, when a prayer need is brought to our attention, we are to immediately pray. We can then keep on praying whenever God brings this need to our mind, until we know an answer has come. When it is possible for you, if the person in need of prayer is with you, put a hand on his shoulder, or join hands with her, lifting up this person and need in prayer right then. *Dear brothers and sisters, pray for us* (1 Thessalonians 5:25).

4. Encourage one another. In this broken world, trials and hardships can often come to us. God puts us in local church families, at least in part so we might lovingly encourage one another through life, especially when facing difficulties.

I cannot begin to list the number of times I have found encouragement from the Lord through sweet fellowship with brothers and sisters in Christ. As a shepherd of God's own flock, I have witnessed again and again Christians coming alongside one another in love, strengthening each other through loving actions and encouraging words. Encouragement is a beautiful gift to see and receive, and our Lord desires to see it in our churches. *Encourage each other and build each other up, just as you are already doing* (1 Thessalonians 5:11).

Jesus would raise up in every local church Christians who will be like the man named Joseph in the early church of Jerusalem. The apostles gave to him a beautiful nickname that described what they all saw in him. He was known in the church for encouragement, so they called him *Barnabas (which means "Son of Encouragement")* (Acts 4:36). Encouraging one another in the church is loving one another.

5. Honor one another. We can show appreciation for each other in the church by speaking words of honor and showing respect and high regard when it is due. We can honor one another for a job well done, for considerate actions, for perseverance, or for faithful living.

Can you think of a time when you were honored, and someone spoke of your significant value to your family or team? Did they thank you for something you did or for a contribution you made? Did you feel affirmed, appreciated, and loved?

Our motivation for doing Christian ministry is not to obtain affirmation or recognition from others, but to faithfully serve Jesus. Yet we can all benefit and be blessed by the loving appreciation that comes with being honored.

Honoring others is love because it serves to affirm, motivate, inspire, uplift, and invigorate. Honoring one another in love can help those who may feel insignificant or forgotten to know they are truly treasured and remembered. Some who have been tempted to quit might then arise with renewed determination.

Honoring one another is not a small matter. God may use this to bring transformation to or in someone. This is why God directs us to lovingly honor one another. Members of our Lord's church are to be prayerfully open, looking for those whom the Lord would have us honor in His name, and to do so with delight. *Love each other with genuine affection, and take delight in honoring each other* (Romans 12:10).

6. Forgive one another. Forgiveness is a priceless gift of grace and love that has been made possible for us by the wonderful grace and love of God in Jesus Christ. If it were not for God's forgiveness, we would have no hope at all. But in great love, God the Father sent God the Son, the Lord Jesus Christ, to make a way for forgiveness of our sins. And we who have received such loving forgiveness are now enabled and blessed to love one another by forgiving one another.

In the Church of Jesus Christ, members who are united with Him through faith are thereby united with one another also. We then demonstrate our true union with Jesus Christ by extending grace to each other as He has extended it to us. This includes forgiving one another as we have been forgiven. Knowing we will need God's help to do this, our Lord taught us to keep praying in this way: *Forgive us our sins, as we have forgiven those who sin against us* (Matthew 6:12).

The foundation of a forgiving spirit in the heart of Christians originates in the experience of receiving through faith the divine grace that is ours in Jesus Christ. After all, it is true that *God saved you by his grace when you believed. And you can't take credit for this; it is a gift from God* (Ephesians 2:8).

It is therefore true that it is only by grace that we now live, and it is by grace that we have been forgiven. Therefore, forgiving one another manifests our true gratitude to God for the great grace we have received in Jesus Christ. *Make allowance for each other's faults and forgive anyone who offends you. Remember, the Lord forgave you, so you must forgive others* (Colossians 3:13).

7. Speak truth to one another. As God's own image-bearers, we can show love to one another by speaking truth, even when it is hard to say or hard to hear. Speaking truth reflects the love of God, who is the *God of truth* (Isaiah 65:16).

In the New Testament, Jesus embodied truth, declaring of Himself, *I am the way, the truth, and the life* (John 14:6). Jesus's life and teachings exemplified truthfulness. Jesus also referred to the Holy Spirit as the *Spirit of truth* (John 16:13) who guides the church to discern truth from falsehood.

Such divine help is crucial in this world that is so filled with deception. Members of Christ's Church are to uphold truth in all areas of life, empowered by the Holy Spirit and guided by the teaching and example of Jesus. This means that *we will not be influenced when people try to trick us with lies so clever they sound like the truth. Instead, we will speak the truth in love, growing in every way more and more like Christ, who is the head of his body, the church* (Ephesians 4:14-15).

To review, seven ways through which local churches can love one another are:

- Gathering with one another
- Living in community with one another
- Praying for one another
- Encouraging one another
- Honoring one another
- Forgiving one another
- Speaking truth to one another

For personal reflection: For each one of these seven ways for local church members to demonstrate love for one another, what is an action the Lord wants you to take in order to love somebody in this manner?

For local church leaders' discussion: For each of these seven ways, what is one action you or your congregation might take that could strengthen your love for one another?

B. Church members follow Jesus

Following Jesus includes going wherever He leads us, even where we hesitate to go. It is doing whatever He requires of us, even when at first we would rather not. It is saying everything He calls us to say, even when we hesitate to say it. Following Jesus means going wherever, doing whatever, and saying whatever, and whenever, He leads us.

Nowhere in the gospels do we see Jesus's true disciples responding to His invitation to follow Him by asking, "To where?" Christian discipleship includes trusting Jesus enough to willingly follow wherever and however He leads.

God has blessed me to live this way. My Lord has led me to places I never dreamed of going when I was a boy or young man. Yes, there have been times when I at first resisted His calling out of fear of the unknown or of the sacrifices that I knew would be required. But my Lord has taught me to trust and obey Him, and by God's grace I have been very privileged to serve in Jesus's name in countless places – in the air, on land, on the sea, and even under the sea. I have been very honored to serve my Lord on five continents and on many islands and in many nations. God has directed me to astounding places, amazing people, and surprising assignments.

It has been my great joy to follow Jesus, who always leads us well, but I can attest that following Jesus means knowing that He sometimes surprises us. But that must be okay with us, because we know He is Lord, and we are not. Although God's direction might not seem right to us at first, we can always know in faith that His ways are good, and so we will choose to follow Him wherever and however He leads. *"My thoughts are nothing like your thoughts," says the* Lord. *"And my ways are far beyond anything you could imagine. For just as the heavens are higher than the earth, so my ways are higher than your ways and my thoughts higher than your thoughts"* (Isaiah 55:8-9).

As career fishermen, Simon, Andrew, James, and John knew how to catch fish. But at the start of their discipleship (as described in Luke 5:1-11), and then again shortly before Jesus ascended to heaven (as told in John 21:1-14), Jesus called His disciples to trust and obey Him by fishing in ways they neither expected nor would have ever chosen to do.

In Luke's account, we see Peter pushing back at first, as Jesus's direction made no sense to him. But Jesus was teaching an especially important lesson that He wanted all of His followers to learn. He teaches us to trust and obey Him, even when His leading makes no sense to our natural minds. *"Master," Simon replied, "we worked hard all last night and did not catch a thing. But if you say so, I'll let the nets down again." And this time their nets were so full of fish they began to tear!* (Luke 5:5-6).

And again after years of following Jesus, learning to love Him, and witnessing His teachings, miracles, and glorious resurrection, these fishermen again followed His surprising instructions, despite their uncertainties. John gave his firsthand account of what occurred that morning, not long after Jesus had risen from the grave:

> *Simon Peter said, "I'm going fishing."*
>
> *"We'll come, too," they all said. So they went out in the boat, but they caught nothing all night. At dawn Jesus was standing on the beach, but the disciples could not see who he was. He called out, "Fellows, have you caught any fish?"*
>
> *"No," they replied.*
>
> *Then he said, "Throw out your net on the right-hand side of the boat, and you'll get some!" So they did, and they couldn't haul in the net because there were so many fish in it.*
>
> *Then the disciple Jesus loved said to Peter, "It's the Lord!" When Simon Peter heard that it was the Lord, he put on his tunic (for he had stripped for work), jumped into the water, and headed to shore. The others stayed with the boat and pulled the loaded net to the shore, for they were only about a hundred yards from shore. When they got there, they found breakfast waiting for them—fish cooking over a charcoal fire, and some bread.*
>
> *"Bring some of the fish you've just caught," Jesus said. So Simon Peter went aboard and dragged the net to the shore. There were 153 large fish, and yet the net hadn't torn.*

"Now, come and have some breakfast!" Jesus said.
(John 21:3-12)

At the beginning of their time following Jesus, and here again near the end of His physical time with them, Jesus taught them, and teaches us, to follow Him and to do whatever He directs us to do. Jesus wants us to learn to trust His guidance, even in those times when it seems to make no earthly sense to us. Jesus wants His disciples to trust and obey Him, even when His leading seems confusing or hard, or when it is not what we would have chosen.

Jesus Christ, who loves us so, calls all members of His Church to make a bold faith decision as our way of life now, to henceforth believe in Him, and to trust and follow Him whenever, wherever, and however He leads us. He wants us to do this willingly and with a heart of love.

A particular aspect of church members loving and following Jesus no matter how He leads us bears special mention here. It concerns the nature of the relationship that the Lord desires of the church members toward their church leaders.

Throughout my lifetime of ministry for Jesus in and for local churches, I have seen incredibly positive effects in churches when relationships and actions between local church members and their leaders are healthy and strong. I have also seen devastating effects on a local church and its members when there is disobedience in this regard.

Following Jesus biblically in His local churches requires members to be encouraging, supporting, and following the spiritual leaders God has placed over them. Our Lord says this to members of His local churches through the writer of the book of Hebrews: *Remember your leaders who taught you the word of God. Think of all the good that has come from their lives, and follow the example of their faith* (Hebrews 13:7).

This directive is further emphasized in this instruction: *Obey your spiritual leaders, and do what they say. Their work is to watch over your souls, and they are accountable to God* (Hebrews 13:17).

For personal reflection: What has it meant in your own life to follow Jesus? Where and when have you gone where Jesus led you, even where you hesitated to go? How have you been blessed through obedience?

How faithfully, and in what ways, have you prayed for, supported, and followed local church leaders as they follow Christ Jesus?

For local church leaders' discussion: What does it mean for you as church leaders to follow Jesus together, setting an example to the church as to what this means? What are some ways your local church intentionally makes disciples who follow Jesus?

C. Church members serve like Jesus

We have been called by the Lord Jesus to serve God, one another, and all to whom He leads us who do not yet know Him. Again, we see the Lord exhibiting and teaching self-effacing service by humbly taking a towel and basin of water and then shocking His disciples by doing what only a servant would do. The Lord of heaven and earth, their Messiah and ours, washed filthy feet! Then this happened:

> *After washing their feet, he put on his robe again and sat down and asked, "Do you understand what I was doing? You call me 'Teacher' and 'Lord,' and you are right, because that's what I am. And since I, your Lord and Teacher, have washed your feet, you ought to wash each other's feet. I have given you an example to follow. Do as I have done to you. I tell you the truth, slaves are not greater than their master. Nor is the messenger more important than the one who sends the message. Now that you know these things, God will bless you for doing them.* (John 13:12-17)

Throughout my lifetime of ministry in the Church of Jesus Christ, in every local church I have been part of, I have known followers of Jesus who demonstrated a servant heart like this. I have known dear brothers and sisters in Jesus Christ who see a need in the church family and respond with the Christlike heart of a servant. It is a beautiful thing to see, for it reflects Jesus. Church members are called to live under Jesus's headship in this way. A good place to begin is to prayerfully consider this question: Have I been more interested in serving or in being served?

When teaching His disciples to have servant hearts like Him, Jesus said this about Himself: *For even the Son of Man came not to be served but to serve others and to give his life as a ransom for many* (Matthew 20:28). Church members who truly want to be like Jesus will want to have servant hearts like Jesus.

A schoolteacher asked her young students, "What do you do to help at home?" One child said, "I wash or dry dishes." Another said, "I sweep the floor." Another said, "I fold laundry." Every child in the class mentioned something they contributed except one boy who was sitting in the back. The teacher called him by name and asked, "What do you do to help at home?" He said, "I stay out of the way."

Faithful church members cannot be content to stay out of the way. Jesus calls all of us to follow His example with servant hearts. If you do not have such a heart, please pray for it. Look for needs around you and do what you can to make a positive difference, whether it is washing dishes, washing floors, stacking chairs, cleaning dirty feet, holding a baby, or whatever else is needed. *Whatever you do or say, do it as a representative of the Lord Jesus, giving thanks through him to God the Father* (Colossians 3:17).

For personal reflection: Who has demonstrated for you a good example of having a servant heart like Jesus? How are you, or how could you, serve like Jesus in your local church?

For local church leaders' discussion: What does it mean for you as church leaders to serve like Jesus, setting an example to the church of what Christlike service means? What are some ways your local church is serving one another, and serving your community, as representatives of Jesus?

D. Church members pray like Jesus

We are to pray as Jesus taught us to pray. Living a Christian life and fulfilling His purposes requires each of us and all of us as a local church to devote ourselves to prayer. This is why Jesus taught us to pray through His example and words.

In Luke 11 we have the beautiful account of Jesus's disciples approaching Him to ask Him to teach them to pray. They wanted to pray like

He did. It was not that they had never prayed, for of course they did. But after following Him for some time, watching and listening to Jesus pray with observable fervency, faith, and power, they undoubtedly discussed it among themselves and agreed that they had much to learn from Jesus about praying. Wanting to pray like Jesus, they asked Him to teach them; and He did. He will do the same for us. *Once Jesus was in a certain place praying. As he finished, one of his disciples came to him and said, "Lord, teach us to pray, just as John taught his disciples"* (Luke 11:1).

This is where we find Jesus teaching the pattern commonly referred to as the "Lord's Prayer." He continued teaching about the importance of prayer to His disciples then, and He teaches local churches the same today. *Jesus told his disciples a story to show that they should always pray and never give up* (Luke 18:1).

Later, when praying in the garden of Gethsemane before He gave His life for us on the cross of suffering, Jesus warned His disciples about the urgency of prayer. He said what we have come to know: *Keep watch and pray, so that you will not give in to temptation. For the spirit is willing, but the body is weak!* (Matthew 26:41).

The Bible says the early church *devoted themselves to . . . prayer* (Acts 2:42). Paul often called the churches to pray. To the local church in Colossae, he urged, *Devote yourselves to prayer with an alert mind and a thankful heart* (Colossians 4:2). To the local church in Thessalonica, he urged, *Never stop praying. Be thankful in all circumstances, for this is God's will for you who belong to Christ Jesus* (1 Thessalonians 5:17-18).

It is important for local churches to pause from time to time to examine their personal and corporate prayer lives. If we would go to a physician for a physical examination, he or she may do various things to measure our relative health. Having faced many health challenges through the years, I understand the importance of such tests and practices, as these have been key in my own evaluations and treatment. Blood labs, EKGs, cardiac stress tests, lung function tests, X-rays, CT scans, EEGs, MRIs, biopsies, and many other methods of medical evaluation can be helpful in evaluating physical health. All of these diagnostic measures have been useful in measuring, addressing, and improving my own physical health, for which I give thanks to God.

Similarly, prayer practices of a local church are a measure of that church's spiritual health. This can be assessed by examining prayer habits of the congregation. I have been to a good many local churches in which little prayer happens in corporate worship services, in the meetings of church leadership teams, or when important decisions are being made by the congregation. This is not God's way for us.

Are there ever meetings when members gather only to pray and to seek God's face, and do members come? Are there any gatherings of small groups who devote themselves to pray for one another, for the church and its leaders, for needs in the community and beyond, for missionaries around the world, and for the growth of His Church? Are prayer warriors mobilized when urgent needs arise? Are there opportunities for people to request and receive prayer whenever the church gathers? Are all decisions faced by the local church leaders and by the congregation being bathed in prayer, always desiring and asking the Lord to lead?

Whenever the prayer life of a local church is measured and found lacking, we must make that a matter of prayer. Ask Jesus for wisdom and guidance in how to proceed. He will surely show us, as promised, if we ask in faith. *If you need wisdom, ask our generous God, and he will give it to you. He will not rebuke you for asking. But when you ask him, be sure that your faith is in God alone* (James 1:5-6).

Church leaders must always remember that the congregation can only go where its leaders will lead them. Leading in prayer means we ourselves pray as a way of life. It means faith-filled conversations with God, committing ourselves, our families, our church life, and all that we do to the Lord.

Together as church leaders, let us ask our Lord to show us how we can make prayer an increasing part of our church life together. This is a prayer God will surely answer.

For personal reflection: How is your prayer life now, and how can you strengthen it?

For local church leaders' discussion: How do you assess the current health of your church's prayer life? What specific things could you do to strengthen the prayer life of the church, devoting yourselves as a congregation to prayer?

E. Church members seek Jesus

Church members are to seek after God and His kingdom, always doing so in the unity of the Holy Spirit. Jesus instructed us to *seek the Kingdom of God above all else, and live righteously, and he will give you everything you need* (Matthew 6:33).

A little later, Jesus gave us this invitation and promise: *Keep on asking, and you will receive what you ask for. Keep on seeking, and you will find. Keep on knocking, and the door will be opened to you. For everyone who asks, receives. Everyone who seeks, finds. And to everyone who knocks, the door will be opened* (Matthew 7:7-8).

Seeking Jesus includes desiring His will and listening to His voice. In his book *Just Like Jesus*, Max Lucado tells of when CBS anchor Dan Rather asked Mother Teresa what she said during her prayers. She answered, "I listen." Turning the question around, Dan Rather asked her, "Well then, what does God say?" To that, Mother Teresa smiled and answered, "He listens."[8]

Her point that day, and my point now, is not that we should fail to use words when we pray, but that seeking the Lord requires our intentionality – truly desiring to hear God, and knowing in faith that God hears us. And as church members are seeking after God, we are to do so together in the unity of the Holy Spirit. This includes desiring, humbly asking, and in faith expecting God to bring His church to unity as we desire God's will.

> *I appeal to you, dear brothers, and sisters, by the authority of our Lord Jesus Christ, to live in harmony with each other. Let there be no divisions in the church. Rather, be of one mind, united in thought and purpose* (1 Corinthians 1:10). *Be patient with each other, making allowance for each other's faults because of your love. Make every effort to keep yourselves united in the Spirit, binding yourselves together with peace. For there is one body and one Spirit, just as you have been called to one glorious hope for the future* (Ephesians 4:2-4).

---

8   Max Lucado, *Just Like Jesus* (Nashville: Thomas Nelson, 2012), 71.

Being members of the Lord's Church means standing together in faith, believing God can and will make possible what seems to be humanly impossible. We are seeking the one who can do all things, knowing that unlike sinful humankind, God can never be confused or divided. The Holy Spirit enables diverse members of Christ's Church to discern and do His will as they seek Him together in faith.

By the Lord's design, members of local churches are not all the same. We have different experiences and perspectives. But because the Lord is never divided or confused, then if and when we are not united in the local church, we are to avoid arguments and vain attempts to prove that we are right and others are wrong. Instead, when the church is not united, we are called and blessed to pray. We are all to humbly lay aside personal agendas and opinions, desiring and seeking only the will of our Lord Jesus Christ. As we do this together, we are able and blessed to ask, expect, and receive the spiritual unity that the Holy Spirit brings.

Seeking Jesus and His will does not consistently happen in the church. It requires determination, discipline, and faith-prompted action. It requires our effort. This is why the apostle Paul exhorted members of the church of Ephesus to *make every effort to keep yourselves united in the Spirit, binding yourselves together with peace* (Ephesians 4:3).

For personal reflection: What are some things you did, said, thought, or prayed in the past year or in the past week out of deep desire and longing for the Lord? What changes might come into your life if you were to seek God with a whole heart, and with others in the unity of the Holy Spirit?

For local church leaders' discussion: How do you assess the current strength of your local church's yearning for God, and what is some evidence for your assessment? What specific things could you do to help the members of your local church seek hard after God, and in the unity of the Holy Spirit?

F. Church members connect with other followers of Jesus
In Christ, we are spiritually united with all who have been washed in His blood through faith in Him, trusting Him for salvation. He has

made us one Church. Again, this theme is evident in Paul's letter to the diverse members of the local church in Ephesus: *There is one body and one Spirit, just as you have been called to one glorious hope for the future. There is one Lord, one faith, one baptism, one God and Father of all, who is over all, in all, and living through all* (Ephesians 4:4-6).

Seven times in this one sentence we hear the word "one," showing that Jesus sees His worldwide Church as one. He therefore desires members to see the Church as He sees it – that we are one with each other in the local church, with Christians in our local area, and with Christians around the world.

God wants us to unite in Him as one family, for we are brothers and sisters in Jesus Christ, now and forever. Can followers of Jesus connect with each other in His name, despite our various denominations, cultures, languages, and nations?

The answer to this is "yes." We can do so because Jesus Christ has made us one in Him. Whenever we connect with other Christians in shared love and ministry, we are living now what will be forever so in heaven, because of God's grace in Jesus.

Leaders and members of local churches therefore honor Jesus by prayerfully seeking, finding, and making ways to connect with other Christians. We can do this by praying with and for them, and by working alongside of and supporting brothers and sisters of local churches in the wider body of Christ. We connect with one another because the Lord Jesus, who is the head of His whole Church, including every true local church, has already connected us with God and one another, uniting us as one in Him.

For personal reflection: When and in what ways have you viewed yourself as connected with other Christians in the wider body of Christ? How can you do so even more?

For local church leaders' discussion: What are some ways your local church has been seeking or showing connections with other churches in the wider body of Christ? What specific things could you do to increase or strengthen such connections?

Chapter 5

Essential Faith Convictions of Historic Biblical Governance

The faith of biblical Christians is rooted in the Bible, the inspired and infallible written Word of God. What we have examined thus far is gleaned from God's special revelation in the Bible. We have considered the three primary levels of authority and responsibility in all biblical local churches: (1) the headship of Jesus Christ over His church, (2) leadership of local church leaders who yield to Jesus's lordship, oversee His church as His under-shepherds, and serve as Jesus did, and (3) membership of local church Christians who are answering His call to love, follow, serve, pray, seek, and connect with other Christians in His name.

From the time of the apostles and the early days of the Church, there has been agreement that in the Church of Jesus Christ, there must be adherence to theological truth as revealed and taught by the Lord and His apostles. The New Testament also shows us that early on, followers of Jesus disagreed about some things that divided the Church. During these times, rather than presuming that truth was to be determined through argument or debate, the Church gathered key leaders together to prayerfully consider what Jesus taught and what the Holy Spirit revealed as they sought the Lord together.

A first example of this is described in Acts 15, when a council convened in Jerusalem to discern whether or not circumcision was to be a requirement for obtaining salvation, as some Jewish leaders were teaching. The Bible describes the strong division that was occurring between people who were convinced that their opinion was right.

The apostles and church elders considered this matter together, recalling what Jesus taught and did, reviewing what the Old Testament Scriptures taught and foretold, and observing what God was now revealing through the outpouring of the Holy Spirit among the gentiles who were being saved. Having prayerfully discerned God's will together, His truth was written, disseminated, and proclaimed to churches: *Then the apostles and elders together with the whole church in Jerusalem chose delegates and they sent them to Antioch in Syria with Paul and Barnabas to report on this decision* (Acts 15:22).

A primary point seen here is that God reveals His truth to those who seek to know and love Him, learning from His Word. It is very important for all people of God, and especially for the leaders of His churches, to seek to know and live according to God's revealed truth. Whenever we do this, we are blessed. If or when we do not do it, we inherit hard consequences of confusion and division.

As Church history progressed, more heresies began to appear, causing arguments and division about what the truth is. Because God can never be divided, and because Jesus Christ, the head of the Church, is Himself ultimate truth, early Church councils convened to address these arguments, to stop the false teachings, and to rightly discern the truth of God.

Because believing and accepting the truth and authority of the Bible is so vitally important in the life of followers of Christ and in His local churches, a brief review is in order of how God gave us the Bible, confirming its authenticity to the Church. The first recorded council of the Christian Church occurred in AD 325, in the ancient city of Nicaea, which is now called Iznik, in Turkey.

This council was called by the Roman emperor Constantine, who believed that a general council of the Lord's church seeking Him together could resolve a growing heresy called Arianism. Arius of Alexandria was promulgating a false teaching that Jesus was not truly divine but was a created being.

That council of church leaders remembered and reviewed the truth that was taught by Jesus, as confirmed in Old Testament scriptures and in acknowledged writings of apostles. They also reviewed writings of esteemed early Church leaders. The council convened with more than three hundred Church leaders from around the known world. Mike del Rosario describes this historic council and its lessons. He said that the Nicene Creed is:

A collaborative statement of essential Christian beliefs compiled from Scripture in 325 AD. This creed was based on the Apostle's Creed and various Scriptures. Early creeds are a good reminder that the essentials of the Christian faith were not created recently, but go back to the earliest memories of Jesus and the teachings of his official spokespeople."[9]

When the council was agreed that they had rightly understood Christ's truth and will, they wrote and published the Nicene Creed. The context and teachings of that council have been thoroughly described in numerous studies, including in a recent book by Jared Ortiz and Daniel Keating, who describe why the process that was followed and the determinations that were made by this and other early Church councils as articulated in early creeds can be helpful to churches today. They wrote:

Why would we bother with creeds in our day? Aren't they just relics from a past age? People today are less and less concerned with truth, and no one seems inclined to follow any authority, especially if that authority is imposed on them from the outside. We could say that our age has taken aim at truth and wants either to obliterate the idea of truth or render it so weak that it has no force in our lives. . . . Our view is that these apparently unfavorable conditions are exactly what make the creeds so crucial for our times. Through their densely packed summaries of the Christian faith, the creeds are precisely the medicine we need. Because we live in an age that doubts the very reality of truth, and because we are trained to go our own way and encouraged to craft our "own truth," we need more than ever an anchor of Truth – given, tested and secure – not just as individuals but together as the church. To our culture the creeds implicitly say, "These things are true and real."[10]

---

9   Mikel Del Rosario, "The Essential Truths of Jesus in the Nicene Creed," October 6, 2017, https://reasonsforjesus.com/the-essential-truths-of-jesus-in-the-nicene-creed/.

10   Jared Ortiz and Daniel A. Keating, *Nicene Creed: A Scriptural, Historical, and Theological Commentary* (Ada, MI: Baker Academic, 2024), 1.

This is what the Holy Spirit does when His Church is seeking His truth together. Jesus promised that when the Holy Spirit is poured out upon the Church, He will guide us into truth: *When the Spirit of truth comes, he will guide you into all truth. He will not speak on his own but will tell you what he has heard. He will tell you about the future. He will bring me glory by telling you whatever he receives from me* (John 16:13-14).

Later, in his letter to the church of Corinth, Paul taught that the Holy Spirit has been given to reveal God's truth to us:

> *But it was to us that God revealed these things by his Spirit. For his Spirit searches out everything and shows us God's deep secrets. No one knows a person's thoughts except that person's own spirit, and no one can know God's thoughts except God's own Spirit. And we have received God's Spirit (not the world's spirit), so we can know the wonderful things God has freely given us. When we tell you these things, we do not use words that come from human wisdom. Instead, we speak words given to us by the Spirit, using the Spirit's words to explain spiritual truths.* (1 Corinthians 2:10-13)

The Holy Spirit planned and breathed out the inspired words of Scripture. With His Church in mind, God then orchestrated the process of rightly discerning which of the early writings of His Church were to be included in the canon.

The word "canon" means "measuring rod." The Holy Spirit stimulated the process for the church to rightly determine the canon of the Bible by discerning which of these books were in fact divinely inspired, and therefore an authoritative part of God's "measuring rod" for His Church.

There was far less controversy over the canon of the Old Testament than of the New Testament. By AD 250, there was almost universal agreement on the canon of the Hebrew Scriptures. The only remaining issue was the Apocrypha, which a vast majority of Hebrew scholars considered to contain good historical and religious documents, but not on the same level of inspiration as the Hebrew Scriptures.

Concerning the New Testament canon, the process of recognition and collection began in the first centuries of the Christian Church.

Exceedingly early, some New Testament books were widely recognized. Paul considered Luke's writings to be as authoritative as the Old Testament, as evidenced, for example, in 1 Timothy 5:18, where he quoted Deuteronomy 25:4 and Luke 10:7: *For the Scripture says, "You must not muzzle an ox to keep it from eating as it treads out the grain." And in another place, "Those who work deserve their pay!"*

The apostle Peter later recognized and affirmed Paul's writings as Scripture: *And remember, our Lord's patience gives people time to be saved. This is what our beloved brother Paul also wrote to you with the wisdom God gave him—speaking of these things in all of his letters. Some of his comments are hard to understand, and those who are ignorant and unstable have twisted his letters to mean something quite different, just as they do with other parts of Scripture. And this will result in their destruction* (2 Peter 3:15-16).

Early on, some books that were later to become part of the New Testament were being circulated among the churches. For example: *After you have read this letter, pass it on to the church at Laodicea so they can read it, too. And you should read the letter I wrote to them* (Colossians 4:16); and *I command you in the name of the Lord to read this letter to all the brothers and sisters* (1 Thessalonians 5:27).

In *The Canon of Scripture*, F. F. Bruce offered a historic examination of how our Bible came to be, rightly observing that in the references and testimonies of Jesus and His apostles, there was already considerable consensus on the limits of the inspired Old Testament.[11]

Regarding the New Testament canon, F. F. Bruce referred to writings of several of the early Church fathers, observing that the recognized authority of New Testament writings significantly preceded the Church councils that formally affirmed the complete composition of the canon.[12] To name a few, as early as AD 95, Clement of Rome mentioned at least eight of the New Testament books. In AD 108, Polycarp, who had been a disciple of John the apostle, acknowledged fifteen books. In AD 115, Ignatius of Antioch acknowledged seven books, and in AD 185, Irenaeus mentioned twenty-one of the New Testament books.

These historical references indicate that New Testament documents were

---

11   F. F. Bruce, *The Canon of Scripture* (Downers Grove, IL: InterVarsity Press, 1988), 28.
12   Bruce, *Canon*, 121-122.

broadly regarded by the churches to be divinely inspired, and thus canonical, long before formal acknowledgment by the Church councils. Still, F. F. Bruce lists and explains the six criteria for New Testament books to be confirmed by the early Church. These were (1) apostolic authority, (2) antiquity, (3) orthodoxy, (4) catholicity, (5) traditional use, and (6) inspiration.[13]

Both the Council of Hippo (AD 393) and the Council of Carthage (AD 397) affirmed the same twenty-seven New Testament books. They carefully discerned whether a book was in fact inspired by the Holy Spirit by determining whether its author was clearly an apostle or closely connected to one, if the book was widely accepted by the Body of Christ, if it was doctrinally orthodox, and if it reflected the revealed character of God in moral and spiritual values.

Because of this prayerful and careful process, it is untrue to suggest that it was the Church or early Church councils that determined the canon of the Bible. It was God who determined the canon of the Bible. God the Holy Spirit imparted knowledge and discernment to leaders of His Church as they prayerfully sought Him together in unity.

We do know firsthand that all humans sin, and it is clearly stated in God's Word: *For everyone has sinned: we all fall short of God's glorious standard* (Romans 3:23). We may therefore rightly presume that the process of collecting and compiling the inspired books of the Bible was not consistently smooth. There would have been some disagreements among devout followers of Jesus whose opinions differed, just as there can be in churches now. But God's sovereignty, the leading of the Holy Spirit, and the unity that appeared in the church councils, with men who prayerfully gathered for this purpose, give confirmation of God's leading in establishing the canon of the Bible.

With the Bible as our guide, we will prayerfully consider six fundamental faith convictions that have always been and still are central beliefs of biblical leaders and local churches. These six faith convictions can be applied in all cultures and eras of history:

1. God's Word is primary.

2. Jesus Christ is Lord.

---

13   Bruce, *Canon*, 256-263.

3. Jesus is the only way to salvation.

4. Every local church is under the direct headship of Jesus Christ.

5. Local churches depend on the presence and power of the Holy Spirit.

6. Local churches are connected with other churches in faith and mission.

God's Word Is Primary

The Bible, the written word of God, is infallible and authoritative, and so is of greater value to the churches than all earthly treasures or praise. The Bible is our authoritative standard for faith and practice because it is God's special revelation of Himself to His people. The doctrine of the Bible's infallibility flows out of God's flawless character. Because God is perfect and true, of necessity His self-revelation is too. God says that His Word always accomplishes what He intends: *The rain and snow come down from the heavens and stay on the ground to water the earth. They cause the grain to grow, producing seed for the farmer and bread for the hungry. It is the same with my word. I send it out, and it always produces fruit. It will accomplish all I want it to, and it will prosper everywhere I send it* (Isaiah 55:10-11).

The primacy of the Bible is because it is entirely infallible, which is to say it is incapable of being wrong. This is so because God is incapable of being wrong. When biblical Christians and local churches speak of the Bible as being infallible, they mean it is wholly trustworthy and true. The Bible cannot teach error. Convictions about the Bible's infallibility have always been part of Christian belief – but is it provable, or is blind faith required?

As we ourselves are much more than the words we speak, so is the incarnate and eternal Word of God more and greater than the written Word of God. In the gospel of John, the eternal, yet incarnate, Lord Jesus is introduced in this way:

> *In the beginning the Word already existed. The Word was with God, and the Word was God. He existed in the*

beginning with God. God created everything through him,
and nothing was created except through him. The Word gave
life to everything that was created, and his life brought light
to everyone. . . . The Word became human and made his
home among us. He was full of unfailing love and faithful-
ness. And we have seen his glory, the glory of the Father's one
and only Son. (John 1:1-4, 14)

We know that Jesus Christ was and is the only begotten eternal Son of God, the Word of God who became flesh. We have not come to this conviction because it was empirically proved to us or because we are smarter than others and figured it out. Rather, we have come to this conviction by faith, for this is the only way anyone can come to this conclusion.

The questions we all must answer are "Will I choose to believe that the Bible is the Word of God?" and "Will I live my life upon this faith?" Billy Graham is well known for his lifetime of proclaiming the good news of Jesus, but his story of coming to faith in Jesus and to a settled conviction of the truth of the Bible is powerful. His story was beautifully told in the movie titled *Billy: The Early Years of Billy Graham*, and in the book by William Paul McKay and Ken Abraham titled *Billy: The Untold Story of a Young Billy Graham and the Test of Faith that Almost Changed Everything*.

When Billy Graham was a young man, his best friend and partner in evangelistic ministry was Charles Templeton. Together they preached the good news, and many came to faith in Jesus Christ as their Savior. But in time, Templeton walked away from the faith, becoming an avowed atheist. After hearing Templeton's strong arguments, Graham was faced with a faith decision that would determine the course of his life, and the course of millions more. Could he, and would he, decide in faith that the Bible was the authoritative and true Word of God?

Billy Graham told the story of how the matter became settled in his heart. He admitted that he could not answer all of Templeton's questions, and there were many things in the Word of God he did not yet understand and could not fully explain. He rightly concluded that he and no other finite human can understand all of God's truth.

But one day as He sought the Lord with all of his heart, he knew that God was calling him to a faith decision. He said to God, "I accept this as Your Word by faith." He said that this decision completely settled it in his heart, and thereafter whenever he quoted the Bible, he knew he was quoting God's Word! And of course, the central message of God's Word is the saving gospel of Jesus Christ.

The book of Hebrews opens by pointing us to Jesus in this way:

> Long ago God spoke many times and in many ways to our
> ancestors through the prophets. And now in these final days,
> he has spoken to us through his Son. God promised every-
> thing to the Son as an inheritance, and through the Son
> he created the universe. The Son radiates God's own glory
> and expresses the very character of God, and he sustains
> everything by the mighty power of his command. When
> he had cleansed us from our sins, he sat down in the place
> of honor at the right hand of the majestic God in heaven.
> (Hebrews 1:1-3)

That is what the Bible does. It points us to the highest revelation of all – the Lord Jesus Christ, who is the eternal Son of God. Hebrews 11 gives a litany of faithful men and women whose stories were told in the Bible. Their common legacy of faith and their witness to the world pointed forward to the coming of Jesus. *All these people earned a good reputation because of their faith, yet none of them received all that God had prom-ised. For God had something better in mind for us* (Hebrews 11:39-40).

The written Word of God points the Church to Jesus Christ. The faithful ones who have gone before us are urging us to also believe and to faithfully follow Him:

> Therefore, since we are surrounded by such a huge crowd of
> witnesses to the life of faith, let us strip off every weight that
> slows us down, especially the sin that so easily trips us up. And
> let us run with endurance the race God has set before us. We
> do this by keeping our eyes on Jesus, the champion who initi-
> ates and perfects our faith. Because of the joy awaiting him, he

*endured the cross, disregarding its shame. Now he is seated in
the place of honor beside God's throne.* (Hebrews 12:1-2)

Because God Himself is infallible, so is God's revelation of Himself. As
Jesus Christ is wholly perfect in nature, so is His revealed Word. The
Word of God teaches the reliability of Scripture. As the apostles Peter
and Paul each approached the end of their earthly journeys, they both
emphasized to the churches the infallibility of God's Word. Recalling
the glorious transfiguration of Jesus, the apostle Peter said:

*For our Lord Jesus Christ has shown me that I must soon
leave this earthly life, so I will work hard to make sure you
always remember these things after I am gone. For we were
not making up clever stories when we told you about the
powerful coming of our Lord Jesus Christ. We saw his majestic splendor with our own eyes when he received honor and
glory from God the Father. The voice from the majestic glory
of God said to him, "This is my dearly loved Son, who brings
me great joy." We ourselves heard that voice from heaven
when we were with him on the holy mountain.*

*Because of that experience, we have even greater confidence
in the message proclaimed by the prophets. You must pay
close attention to what they wrote, for their words are like
a lamp shining in a dark place—until the Day dawns, and
Christ the Morning Star shines in your hearts. Above all, you
must realize that no prophecy in Scripture ever came from
the prophet's own understanding, or from human initiative.
No, those prophets were moved by the Holy Spirit, and they
spoke from God.* (2 Peter 1:14-21)

Because the Bible is "God-breathed" and is the product of the perfect
and holy God, it can only be true, and completely so. Approaching his
own imminent death, the apostle Paul accentuated to young Timothy
the high priority of believing this:

You must remain faithful to the things you have been taught. You know they are true, for you know you can trust those who taught you. You have been taught the holy Scriptures from childhood, and they have given you the wisdom to receive the salvation that comes by trusting in Christ Jesus. All Scripture is inspired by God and is useful to teach us what is true and to make us realize what is wrong in our lives. It corrects us when we are wrong and teaches us to do what is right. God uses it to prepare and equip his people to do every good work. (2 Timothy 3:14-17)

The Koine Greek word used here by Paul to describe *all Scripture* is "θεόπνευστος" (*theopneustos*). This is a compound word derived from "θεός" (*theos*), meaning "God," and "πνέω" (*pneo*), meaning "to breathe." A literal translation of "θεόπνευστος" is "God-breathed" or "breathed out by God." Though it is translated well as "inspired by God," it means more than a typical use of that word. This image of Scripture being God-breathed reveals God's active and living involvement in creation of the holy Scriptures. The human authors of the Bible were therefore being guided by divine influence.

Besides its claims of infallibility, the Bible's accuracy is supported by inductive reasoning through many sources, including ancient manuscripts, archaeology, and historical studies. Unlike texts of other religions, the Bible has a verifiable historical basis, with cities, geography, nations, and peoples all rooted in real time and history. Biblical stories are not fables. They are accounts of God's works through history.

Particularly significant in discussions about biblical infallibility is the reliable transmission of the biblical manuscripts. Technically, God-breathed inspiration of the Bible pertains to the original autographs. However, a study of the history of the Bible's manuscripts, known as textual criticism, reveals an exceptionally high degree of accuracy in the copying and preservation of the sacred texts.

Between 1946 and 1956, what became known as the Dead Sea Scrolls were discovered by Bedouin shepherds and a team of archaeologists. These were found in a series of twelve caves located near the Dead Sea, in an area then controlled by Jordan. These included about two hundred copies of Old Testament manuscripts dating from more than two thousand years ago, the oldest of which dates from about 200 BC.

In their guidebook *What Are the Dead Sea Scrolls and Why Do They Matter?*, David Noel Freedman and Pam Fox Kuhlken explain the content of the Dead Sea Scrolls, discussing their significance in the context of history and the preservation of biblical texts. Answering the question "Did the Dead Sea Scrolls change the course of biblical scholarship?" they said:

> They changed the course of biblical scholarship in that they prove that the text of the Hebrew Bible that has come down to us is more reliable than previously thought—that fewer scribal or editorial changes or errors had occurred over the centuries than scholars once imagined. They confirm that by 100 B.C. the canon and the text of authoritative books of the Hebrew Bible had been fixed. Despite some small variations, the Dead Sea Scrolls reflect the same selection of books and have very much the same wording as our current Hebrew Bible.[14]

These long-preserved manuscripts reveal the remarkable accuracy of the Hebrew text over many centuries. Such preservation was clearly guided and guarded by God, who gave and has protected this special revelation for the original recipients, and for all peoples and generations, including us and our churches now.

This same carefulness applies to the New Testament, which amazingly has more than five thousand Greek manuscripts and fragments. Some of these fragments are as old as only one generation removed from the originals. Scholars affirm that every original word is included in the text or alternative readings. The New Testament has more early copies than any other ancient writing, providing amazing evidence of its accuracy.

There is much internal evidence of the Bible's infallibility, revealing itself to be extremely accurate. There is also much external evidence supporting the claim that the Bible is unique among all historical texts. It is authoritative and infallible. Because its words are ultimately from God, it is worthy of our devotion, as declared poetically in Psalm 1: *Oh, the joys of those who do not follow the advice of the wicked, or stand*

---

14   David Noel Freedman and Pam Fox Kuhlken, *What Are the Dead Sea Scrolls and Why Do They Matter?* (Grand Rapids: WM. B. Eerdmans Publishing Co., 2007), 4.

around with sinners, or join in with mockers. But they delight in the law of the Lord, *meditating on it day and night. They are like trees planted along the riverbank, bearing fruit each season. Their leaves never wither, and they prosper in all they do* (Psalm 1:1-3).

Faithfully leading and being a local church under the headship of Jesus requires having and sharing this fundamental conviction that God's Word is primary. The Bible is the Word of God written. It is infallible, so for us it is authoritative and greater than all else.

When this conviction is firm in our hearts, it becomes for us a way of life not just personally, but also as families, as leaders, and as local churches. We will therefore want to read, study, preach, pray, learn, meditate, memorize, talk about, and live by what God has revealed in His Word. The Bible is precious to us. *Your instructions are more valuable to me than millions in gold and silver* (Psalm 119:72). *Your word is a lamp to guide my feet and a light for my path* (Psalm 119:105).

For personal reflection: To what degree has God's Word been primary for you, and how is this evident in your way of life? How has the Word of God blessed you?

For local church leaders' discussion: What evidence do you see of the Word of God being primary for the people of your local church? How is your personal and shared conviction about the primacy and authority of the Bible evident in how you are making decisions personally, as a leadership team, and as a church of God's people?

Jesus Christ Is Lord of All

Biblical churches acknowledge and confess that Jesus Christ is Lord of all. The New Testament teaches this truth, which is foundational in biblical local church governance. The apostle Peter said, *This is the message of Good News for the people of Israel—that there is peace with God through Jesus Christ, who is Lord of all* (Acts 10:36).

The title *Lord of all* expresses our belief in Jesus's authority over all creation, over all of His Church (including our local church), and over all of our personal life. This foundational conviction reflects our shared belief in Jesus's divinity and sovereignty, as it is affirmed in God's Word, the Bible.

The apostle Paul stated it this way in his letter to the local church in Philippi: *Therefore, God elevated him to the place of highest honor and gave him the name above all other names, that at the name of Jesus every knee should bow, in heaven and on earth and under the earth, and every tongue declare that Jesus Christ is Lord, to the glory of God the Father* (Philippians 2:9-11).

As Lord of all, Jesus Christ possesses all the attributes of God, including omnipotence, omniscience, and omnipresence. As Lord of all, Jesus is able to do all things for His Church with infinite power, knowledge, and wisdom. As Lord of all, He is the supreme authority we want and need in and for our churches.

As Lord of all and head of His body, the Church, Jesus guides and governs us. In a letter written to a local church, the apostle Paul said, *God has put all things under the authority of Christ and has made him head over all things for the benefit of the church. And the church is his body; it is made full and complete by Christ, who fills all things everywhere with himself* (Ephesians 1:22-23).

This imagery makes it clear that local churches must be fully dependent on Jesus for His leadership. Jesus makes us full and complete. We are fully dependent on the Lord of all for wisdom, direction, unity, and growth. This faith conviction has profound implications for our faith, daily living, and church governance.

I was nineteen years old when I first began to understand what it means that Jesus Christ is Lord of all. This conviction has had powerful implications in my personal life – in His calling me to serve wherever He leads, and in every leadership position He assigns me. Believing that Jesus Christ is Lord of all means desiring Him to be on the throne in my own life and in His churches, holding all authority. This biblical conviction calls for a personal response from every leader and church member in worship, obedience, and submission to His will. For our local churches, having this conviction calls for sharing a commitment to desire and to intently seek the will, leadership, and guidance of Jesus Christ for His church.

How essential is it that we are sharing and declaring this conviction?

If you openly declare that Jesus is Lord and believe in your heart that God raised him from the dead, you will be saved (Romans 10:9).

Having the faith conviction that Jesus Christ is Lord of all allows us to receive His comfort, assurance, and peace – even if and when our circumstances are very difficult. I testified of this glorious truth in the book I wrote when walking through cancer: *Walking with God through Deep Valleys.*[15]

Believing and confessing that Jesus Christ is Lord of all means that we know personally that His good purposes will prevail. As church leaders, we know this too – that no matter what challenges are before us, we can know with certainty that the Lord of all will surely guide us and see us through. And as local churches, we can always know that the Lord of all loves us, has a good plan for us, and will lead us and fulfill His purposes for us. The Lord of all is always to be our deepest love, holding all authority in our personal life and in our churches.

For personal reflection: When and how did you come to believe and confess that Jesus Christ is Lord of all, which includes being Lord of your life? How has this faith conviction affected you through the years and especially more recently?

For local church leaders' discussion: The Bible says, *God has put all things under the authority of Christ and has made him head over all things for the benefit of the church* (Ephesians 1:22). How and to what degree has this conviction been evident in your local church? How does shared conviction of the lordship of Jesus over all things affect the way you approach decisions as a leadership team and as a church?

Jesus Christ Is the Only Way to Salvation

Jesus Christ is not merely one of many possible paths to salvation. If there was any other way, would God have sent His beloved Son to suffer so violently and to die in such agony? What a crazy thought! No righteous and loving person would do such a thing! Yet moved by

---

15   Stephen A. Gammon, *Walking with God through Deep Valleys: Lessons on Finding Contentment When Life Is Hard* (Abbotsford, WI: Aneko Press, 2020).

infinite love, God did just that. God sent Jesus to be our Savior. *For this is how God loved the world: He gave his one and only Son, so that everyone who believes in him will not perish but have eternal life. God sent his Son into the world not to judge the world, but to save the world through him* (John 3:16-17).

God willingly sent Jesus to die in our place as our one way to salvation. Jesus said it this way: *I am the way, the truth, and the life. No one can come to the Father except through me* (John 14:6).

Because of this absolute truth, biblical local churches should always be praying as Jesus exhorted us, saying, *The harvest is great, but the workers are few. So pray to the Lord who is in charge of the harvest; ask him to send more workers into his fields* (Matthew 9:37). This conviction is of high importance in local churches because the Bible teaches what we have come to know – that Jesus truly is the only way of salvation.

There are many people who profess to be followers of Jesus, yet who refuse to accept what He taught – that He is the only way to everlasting life. There are many local churches that believe and teach that there are many paths to God and eternal life.

My wife, Helen, describes a local church in which she grew up in which her youth leader insisted that everyone would be saved, no matter what they believed, saying that there are countless roads to the same destination. When Helen came to personal faith in Jesus Christ for her salvation, the Lord led her away from that place where a false gospel was being preached. She was led to a local church that believed that the Bible was true, that Jesus Christ is Lord of all, and that He is the one and only way of salvation.

When I served as a local church pastor, I always aimed to establish personal relationships with other local churches and clergy. One way I did this was by attending meetings of local church ministers. At one monthly meeting that I attended not long after I had moved into a new community, I was astounded by what I heard. Several clergy were expressing their anger and dismay because of letters they heard about that had been sent out by leaders of a particular Christian denomination. In that letter, ministers and local churches were called to specifically pray for the salvation of adherents of various religions that were listed. When I heard the discussion among the clergy that day, my heart ached deeply because no one was expressing an understanding of the absolute necessity of the gospel of Jesus.

As I listened, I began to pray, asking God to open the eyes of the spiritually blind. Approaching the end of that meeting, someone said, "I wish I knew someone who could help me understand where these people are coming from, that they have become so arrogant, bigoted, and narrow." Then I spoke up and said, "I would be glad to do that." I was immediately added to the agenda for the next meeting.

By the time the next monthly clergy meeting arrived, it had been heavily bathed in prayer by me and the other leaders of the church I served. When I was called upon to address the question that was raised the prior month, I led in prayer, asking the Holy Spirit to be our teacher, and to show us Jesus. I then opened the Bible, reviewing the gospel of biblical Christianity. Reading portions from Old and New Testaments, I described the sinfulness of humanity, the consequences of sin, humankind's need, and God's great promise of a Savior who would be for us *the Lamb of God who takes away the sin of the world* (John 1:29). I showed that this promise, often foretold by God, was strung like a golden thread through the Old Testament, as, for example, in Genesis 2:15, Exodus 12:11-13; Exodus 29:38-42, Jeremiah 11:19, and Isaiah 53:7. I also referred to several verses in the Gospels showing that this was precisely what Jesus said He was going to do, as in Mark 10:45, Matthew 28:28, John 3:14-15, John 8:24, and John 10:11, 15.

I then read verses from New Testament epistles that clearly stated that salvation is made possible solely by God's grace, through our faith in Jesus Christ. I said that His essential sacrifice for us was the central message of the church since the beginning, as seen in Romans 3:23, Romans 5:8, 10, Romans 6:23, 1 Corinthians 15:3, 1 Corinthians 15:17, 2 Corinthians 5:21, Galatians 2:20, Ephesians 2:8-9, Colossians 2:14, 1 Peter 2:24, and 1 Peter 3:18.

My reasoned explanation for why followers of Jesus pray and evangelize was because it is the only natural outflow of believing what the Bible has revealed and what historic Christianity has taught – that God's Word is authoritative and infallible, and that Jesus Christ truly is Lord of all. These convictions lead us to understand and believe that Jesus was, is, and forevermore will be the one and only way to salvation.

I recall quoting Jesus that day, who said concerning Himself, *I am the way, the truth, and the life. No one can come to the Father except through me* (John 14:6). I reminded the clergy that it would be irrational to presume that anyone who truly holds these historic convictions could in good conscience fail to evangelize. I said that it would, in fact, be unloving and unfaithful to fail to care for or pray for those who have not yet come to know and trust in Jesus Christ for their salvation.

After I finished, I entertained many questions. Then I led the group in prayer, thanking God for His Word and for the historic good news of Christianity. I prayed that the Holy Spirit would open our wills to desire His truth, and open our hearts and minds to receive spiritual understanding and to respond in faith.

After our time together that day, an older pastor approached me with tears. He said with observable emotion, "I have attended these meetings for many years. This is the first time I have sensed the presence of God the Holy Spirit among us. Truth was proclaimed today. Christ was exalted. He is the way, the truth, and the life."

Yes. Biblical local churches do believe that the Bible is our authoritative guide, that Jesus Christ is Lord of all, and that He is the one and only way of salvation.

For personal reflection: Have you truly believed and confessed that Jesus Christ is the one and only way of salvation? If not, what has kept you from believing this? If so, how has this faith conviction affected you through the years and especially more recently?

For local church leaders' discussion: To what degree, and how, has the conviction been evident in your local church that Jesus Christ is the one and only way of salvation? What would it look like, and how might it happen, for this biblical truth to become even more real among your members?

Each Local Church Is Under the Direct Headship of Jesus Christ

This truth was considered in the previous chapter about the three levels of authority and responsibility in all biblical local churches: headship, leadership, and membership. I again list the headship of Christ as a fundamental faith conviction of biblical leaders and churches because this conviction is critical to the life and health of local churches. When we lose sight of this, thinking or acting as if the local church belongs to us, with the decisions being "mine" or "ours," then we fail to thrive.

As living branches draw their life from the vine or trunk to which they are attached, and as all living bodies receive direction from the head, so must local churches draw life, motivation, wisdom, direction, and protection from our vine and head, even Christ. Local churches must know that we are under the headship of Jesus.

This fundamental truth is connected to Jesus's teaching in John 15:

> *I am the true grapevine, and my Father is the gardener. He cuts off every branch of mine that does not produce fruit, and he prunes the branches that do bear fruit so they will produce even more. You have already been pruned and purified by the message I have given you. Remain in me, and I will remain in you. For a branch cannot produce fruit if it is severed from the vine, and you cannot be fruitful unless you remain in me. Yes, I am the vine; you are the branches. Those who remain in me, and I in them, will produce much fruit. For apart from me you can do nothing. Anyone who does not remain in me is thrown away like a useless branch and withers. Such branches are gathered into a pile to be burned. But if you remain in me and my words remain in you, you may ask for anything you want, and it will be granted! When you produce much fruit, you are my true disciples. This brings great glory to my Father.* (John 15:1-8)

Christ is the life-giving source of our fruitfulness and of life itself. We could not breathe, and we would not live, if it were not for the love and grace of God in Jesus Christ. Biblical local churches and church leaders believe that our very life is in Jesus Christ. He is our Lord and the head of His body, the Church. Holding this conviction firmly, we aim to live it personally each day, and to do so in life together as a local church.

As we have seen, we will be letting go of any sense of personal ownership, as though this church is mine or ours, or that I or we get to decide what this local church is going to be or do. Because we are under the headship of Jesus, we want Him to lead us however He will.

Living with the fundamental faith conviction that our local church truly is under the direct headship of Jesus Christ is very important for the life, health, growth, and fruitfulness of the church. If at this moment you are not wholly sure that you have personally grasped this, or that together as church leaders you have not firmly grasped this fundamental conviction, then I hope you will read and consider again the lessons above in chapter four on the three levels of authority and responsibility in all biblical local churches. For the church, this can be the difference between fruitfulness and fruitlessness, even between life and death.

In the same way that each life, marriage, family, and home must be built upon a solid foundation if it is to endure and thrive, so must every local church be built on a solid foundation of faith in Christ, who is truly the chief cornerstone and head over all. Hear again and prayerfully meditate on these words spoken by Jesus on this theme of building upon a solid foundation:

> *Anyone who listens to my teaching and follows it is wise, like a person who builds a house on solid rock. Though the rain comes in torrents and the floodwaters rise and the winds beat against that house, it won't collapse because it is built on bedrock. But anyone who hears my teaching and doesn't obey it is foolish, like a person who builds a house on sand. When the rains and floods come and the winds beat against that house, it will collapse with a mighty crash.* (Matthew 7:24-27)

The apostle Paul also wrote in a similar way:

> *God has put all things under the authority of Christ and has made him head over all things for the benefit of the church.* (Ephesians 1:22)

> *Together, we are his house, built on the foundation of the apostles and the prophets. And the cornerstone is Christ Jesus himself. We are carefully joined together in him,*

becoming a holy temple for the Lord. Through him you Gentiles are also being made part of this dwelling where God lives by his Spirit. (Ephesians 2:20-22)

Christ is also the head of the church, which is his body. He is the beginning, supreme over all who rise from the dead. So he is first in everything. (Colossians 1:18)

We must fully realize and put into practice the fundamental faith conviction that each of us personally, and all of us concurrently as a local church, are answerable and accountable to Jesus Christ. He is Lord of all and head over the Church, including each particular local church.

As a local church leader and as a denominational leader, I learned that my responsibility isn't to lead the church in the way I want it to go, or to make decisions based on my own preferences. Neither is it my responsibility to convince others that I am right so that they must agree with me and do whatever I have decided to do.

For the church to truly be led by the Lord Jesus, local church leaders especially must grasp and prayerfully aim to live this biblical concept. We are to continually put our ears to the heart of Jesus, prayerfully listening to hear His heartbeat. We must prayerfully desire to hear His voice so that we might know and do His will.

I have learned that this responsibility is so significant, that as a pastor and ministry leader I must regularly take time to do precisely what Jesus did: *Jesus often withdrew to the wilderness for prayer* (Luke 5:16). Since Jesus often went apart from the busyness and demands of life to put His ear to the Father's heart, surely we need to do the same and have focused seasons of prayer and listening.

I am very glad that as a young pastor, I learned the importance of doing this in my life. A seasoned pastoral mentor encouraged me to do this, and I quickly found the wisdom of doing so. Every three months or so, I went apart for at least one day, and sometimes overnight or for a few days, to seek God's face, listen, and pray. When funds were tight, I asked God to lead me to a free or affordable place to go or stay apart from distractions. He often provided this for me, as this is a prayer He loves to answer.

At times, I engaged with our church leaders in retreat settings for a day or two to listen, pray, and seek God's guidance. This practice fosters a sense of sacred community and shared vision, unified by the Holy Spirit.

I have many precious memories of God meeting me in such personal times, and of meeting church leaders as we went apart to pray and seek His face together. God gave to us whatever was needed then: vision, direction, correction, instruction, comfort, encouragement, peace, and love. When leaders seek Him together like this, the Holy Spirit can bring unity that cannot be achieved in any other way.

We are to humbly and often seek Jesus together, desiring His will and being willing to go wherever He sends us, to say whatever He tells us to say, to do whatever He gives us to do, and to be whatever He would have us be. The Head of the church promises to meet and lead us as we seek Him.

But if we are failing to seek Jesus like this, could it be that we are merely pretending to others that we believe that Jesus is the head of this church? Could it be that we really wish to retain control ourselves?

All local churches that want to be biblical will take very seriously this sacred responsibility of being the Lord's church however He wants to lead them. We will faithfully seek to prayerfully search and listen to the Scriptures, and to hear His voice, in order to rightly discern His will. We will authentically show His love, speak His truth, and do His works. We know in faith that this will happen in this local church because we are under the headship of the Lord Jesus.

For personal reflection: Do you believe that you and your local church are indeed under Jesus's headship? How have you lived out this conviction? Have you lately gone apart to put your ear to God's own heart? If not, why not? If so, what happened?

For local church leaders' discussion: To what degree is this conviction evident among your leadership team? Have you lately gone apart together to put your ear to God's heart? If not, why not? If so, what happened? How is this being lived out in your congregation?

Local Churches Depend upon the Holy Spirit's Presence and Power

The person and presence of the Holy Spirit is revealed in the Bible, was declared in historic Christian creeds, and is confessed in statements of faith of churches that believe and affirm faith in the Trinitarian God. Jared Ortiz and Daniel Keating have done a superb job of describing some of the early church issues of confusion regarding the person and work of the Holy Spirit. This matter was addressed in the Nicene Council and Creed (AD 325) and then clarified further in the Council of Constantinople (AD 381).[16]

Gregory of Nazianzus (AD 329-390) was an early Christian theologian who served as Archbishop of Constantinople from 380-381. He is remembered as the "Trinitarian Theologian" because he, among other key church leaders of his day, was instrumental in helping the Church understand and more clearly articulate the relationship among the three persons of the Trinity.

Nazianzus also provided a reasonable explanation as to why, in the history of God's relational covenants and revelations to humankind, the full person and divinity of the Holy Spirit was more clearly revealed last in order, after the Father and the Son. Nazianzus explained how and why in the progressive revelation of God the Bible first presented the person of God as Father, then at the right time the prophesied person of the Son of God was introduced, and later still the person of God the Holy Spirit was more fully revealed. There surely were prophecies of the Holy Spirit in the Old Testament, with many such references being future-focused, regarding what God would one day reveal and do. For example, *I will give you a new heart, and I will put a new spirit in you. I will take out your stony, stubborn heart and give you a tender, responsive heart* (Ezekiel 36:26).

This prophetic passage, through the prophet Isaiah, was read by Jesus on that day when, in His hometown of Nazareth, He announced its fulfilment at the beginning of His public ministry (see Luke 4:18-19):

> *The Spirit of the Lord GOD is upon me, because the Lord*
> *has anointed me to bring good news to the poor; he has sent*
> *me to bind up the brokenhearted, to proclaim liberty to*

---

16   Ortiz and Keating, *Nicene Creed,* 142-171.

the captives, and the opening of the prison to those who are bound; to proclaim the year of the LORD's favor, and the day of vengeance of our God; to comfort all who mourn; to grant to those who mourn in Zion—to give them a beautiful head-dress instead of ashes, the oil of gladness instead of mourn-ing, the garment of praise instead of a faint spirit; that they may be called oaks of righteousness, the planting of the LORD, that he may be glorified. (Isaiah 61:1-3 ESV)

We also remember the promise made through the prophet Joel that Peter quoted on the day of Pentecost, announcing that this prophecy was fulfilled that very day, as the Holy Spirit was being poured out upon all flesh (see Acts 2:17-18): *I will pour out my Spirit on all people. Your sons and daughters will prophesy. Your old men will dream dreams, and your young men will see visions. In those days I will pour out my Spirit even on servants—men and women alike* (Joel 2:28-29).

Gregory of Nazianzus identified this gradual presentation of the three persons of one God as God's chosen way of educating us about the divine concept and relationships that are within the one person of the triune God. He wrote:

In this way the old covenant made clear presentation of the Father, a less definite one of the Son. The new covenant made the Son manifest and gave us a glimpse of the Spirit's Godhead. At the recent time, the Spirit resides amongst us, giving us a clearer manifestation of Himself than before. It was dangerous for the Son to be preached openly when the Godhead of the Father was still unacknowledged. It was dangerous, too, for the Holy Spirit to be made (here I use a rather rash expression) an extra burden, when the Son had not been received. . . . No, God meant it to be by piece-meal additions, "ascents" as David called them, by prog-ress and advance from glory to glory, that the light of the Trinity should shine upon more illustrious souls. This was, I believe, the motive for the Spirit's making his home in the disciples in gradual stages proportionate to their capacity to receive him.[17]

Reflecting on biblical leaders and local churches, I considered Nazianzus's views on the delayed understanding of God the Holy Spirit. Though I cannot vouch for the accuracy of his theological assessment, it resonates with my own experience and observations in local churches.

An understanding of God as Heavenly Father seemed easier for me to understand, even from early childhood – perhaps because I had an earthly father who loved me and showed his love. People who have not had a loving father still know what a father is and can long for such a relationship of reliable love and trust.

When I was a little child, an understanding of Jesus, the Son of God, was perhaps the easiest person of the Trinity for me to understand and relate to because He, too, entered this world as a baby in human flesh. And Jesus grew up as a child, as we all do, and even in a small town like I did. As the Bible says about Jesus's childhood in the little town of Nazareth, *There the child grew up healthy and strong. He was filled with wisdom, and God's favor was on him* (Luke 2:40).

Jesus taught good news of life and salvation. No one had ever heard anyone like Him before. Even those who opposed Jesus, such as the temple guards sent to arrest Him, were in such awe that they said, *We have never heard anyone speak like this!* (John 7:46).

Jesus Christ, the Son of God, very beautifully and effectively demonstrated the character and power of God in how He lived and loved, healed and gave hope, welcomed and embraced, gave and forgave, and reconciled and restored. Like all of us, Jesus knew sorrow and suffering. I relate with Jesus, for like us, He, too, was human. With love, Jesus sacrificially offered His life in my place. Even as a boy, I knew Jesus personally, and throughout my life I have been blessed to know and love Him.

As Gregory of Nazianzus described the progressive revelation to humankind of God's Trinitarian nature, so my own understanding of the person of the Holy Spirit came after comprehending the persons of God

---

17   Gregory of Nazianzus, "Oration 31.6," in *On God and Christ: The Five Theological Orations and Two Letters to Cledonius,* translated by Lionel Wickham (Crestwood, NY: St. Vladimir Seminary Press 2002), 137.

the Father and God the Son. In my upbringing, I was taught and knew that God is three distinct persons in one being, but I had no understanding of the person of God the Holy Spirit or what it means to relate to Him.

Who can sufficiently explain the nature of the Trinity so that anyone can fully grasp it, much less for a child to understand? Because there is nothing in human experience to compare to this divine concept of one God in three distinct persons, our minds cannot comprehend it. And so many professing Christians simply choose not to believe this truth that the Lord Jesus and the Bible have declared.

The sad truth is that many who regard themselves as followers of Jesus Christ do not believe this biblical doctrine of the Trinity. A recent research report from the Cultural Research Center at Arizona Christian University, led by Dr. George Barna, surprisingly reveals that just 16 percent of self-proclaimed Christians in the United States actually believe in the Trinity.[18] This research shines a light upon the troubling difficulty so many people have with accepting doctrines of historic Christianity as revealed in the Bible.

When I was young, I was taught and I believed in the Holy Trinity, because it is revealed in the Holy Scriptures and in the history of the Church that there is one God who is three distinct persons – the Father, the Son, and the Holy Spirit. But I was not taught, nor did I ever consider, much about the person of God the Holy Spirit. This changed for me when I began hearing Jesus calling me to follow Him and to prepare for shepherding His Church. Soon thereafter, I became personally and wonderfully introduced to the Holy Spirit.

Jesus taught His disciples that they and all who would follow Him would need the Holy Spirit to fill, teach, empower, and enable them for discerning and doing His will. I learned firsthand how great my need was and is for the Holy Spirit to fill, equip, lead, and enable me. This biblical truth applies to every Christian believer and to every local church.

When facing life decisions about what to do next, I often longed and asked for the Holy Spirit to fill and lead me, and He did. When confronting ministry challenges for which I knew I was inadequate in my natural abilities, I often longed and asked for the promised equipping and

---

18 "American Worldview Inventory 2025," conducted by the Cultural Research Center at Arizona Christian University, https://www.arizonachristian.edu/wp-content/uploads/2025/03/AWVI-2025_03_Most-Americans-Reject-the-Trinity_FINAL_03_26_2025.pdf.

anointing of the Holy Spirit. For the praise and glory of God, I testify that the Holy Spirit indeed enabled me for every challenge. Jesus taught us to ask God, our Father, for the gift of the Holy Spirit: *You fathers—if your children ask for a fish, do you give them a snake instead? Or if they ask for an egg, do you give them a scorpion? Of course not! So if you sinful people know how to give good gifts to your children, how much more will your heavenly Father give the Holy Spirit to those who ask him* (Luke 11:11-13).

When prayerfully studying all of this as a young man, I came to realize that I had never done what Jesus specifically instructed me to do. I had never asked my Heavenly Father for the fullness of the good gift of the Holy Spirit to anoint and fill me. I then began praying, asking our Heavenly Father to examine my heart to see if there was anything in me that kept me from desiring and allowing the Holy Spirit to fill and lead me. After confessing the sins that were revealed to me, I humbly asked my Father to fill and anoint me with the Holy Spirit for His glory and purposes, and for my good.

God answered my prayers that day, and a new world was opened to me in my personal relationship with God and in dependency upon God in life and ministry. I began knowing and understanding even more fully the person and power of the Holy Spirit, and my life and ministry were substantively changed.

In my first book, *Walking with God: 101 Lessons for Life and Ministry*, I shared some of the life-changing lessons God has taught me while walking with Him through the years. In lesson 26, titled "God Satisfies the Thirsty with the Holy Spirit," I told my own story of the Holy Spirit becoming very real to me.[19]

Sharing such personal stories of God's grace in our lives must never be done with pride or boasting, but always humbly and with praise to God. After alluding to some glorious experiences and things God had done in his life, the apostle Paul told of how God also blessed him with the physical infirmity of a *thorn in the flesh* to remind and teach him this lesson that all believers and local churches must learn: *"My grace is all you need. My power works best in weakness." So now I am glad to boast about my weaknesses, so that the power of Christ can work through me* (2 Corinthians 12:9).

---

19   Stephen A. Gammon, *Walking with God: 101 Lessons for Life and Ministry* (Abbotsford, WI: Aneko Press, 2014), 66-69.

For many Christians and churches, our weaknesses bring us to realize how very much we need the Holy Spirit, who Christ promised would come. We also see that the same Holy Spirit who comes to all who trust in Jesus Christ does not work in all of us in the same way. The Spirit's gifts are diverse, and we are each uniquely made and gifted by God for our good and for God's glory.

We can also know that the Holy Spirit's work in the life of each disciple and in each of our local churches will always be consistent with the inspired written Word of God. A summary lesson from my own story that I learned and have often shared is that "we should examine our experiences through the filter of Scripture, for God's Word is infallible but our experience is not."[20]

It is very good for us to prayerfully consider again what the Lord Jesus said about this for all of His followers in local churches. We have been wonderfully called, invited, and privileged to be living now and forever in a personal relationship of continued intimacy and dependence upon the Holy Spirit. Our God is still God with us, and the Holy Spirit is now God in us. Jesus taught this glorious truth: *I will ask the Father, and he will give you another Advocate, who will never leave you. He is the Holy Spirit, who leads into all truth. The world cannot receive him, because it isn't looking for him and doesn't recognize him. But you know him, because he lives with you now and later will be in you* (John 14:16-17). Jesus also said:

> *It is best for you that I go away, because if I don't, the Advocate won't come. If I do go away, then I will send him to you. And when he comes, he will convict the world of its sin, and of God's righteousness, and of the coming judgment. The world's sin is that it refuses to believe in me. Righteousness is available because I go to the Father, and you will see me no more. Judgment will come because the ruler of this world has already been judged.*
>
> *There is so much more I want to tell you, but you can't bear it now. When the Spirit of truth comes, he will guide you*

---

20   Gammon, *Walking with God: 101 Lessons*, 67.

into all truth. He will not speak on his own but will tell
you what he has heard. He will tell you about the future.
He will bring me glory by telling you whatever he receives
from me. All that belongs to the Father is mine; this is why I
said, "The Spirit will tell you whatever he receives from me."
(John 16:7-15)

When introducing the "Acts of the Apostles," Luke included the promise
and instructions that Jesus gave concerning the Holy Spirit just prior to
His ascension into heaven. Jesus said that the Holy Spirit would soon
come. Then He instructed His disciples to wait until the Spirit came
upon them in power before going out in His name to preach the good
news, establishing His Church in this world:

In my first book I told you, Theophilus, about everything
Jesus began to do and teach until the day he was taken up
to heaven after giving his chosen apostles further instruc-
tions through the Holy Spirit. During the forty days after he
suffered and died, he appeared to the apostles from time to
time, and he proved to them in many ways that he was actu-
ally alive. And he talked to them about the Kingdom of God.

Once when he was eating with them, he commanded them,
"Do not leave Jerusalem until the Father sends you the gift
he promised, as I told you before. John baptized with water,
but in just a few days you will be baptized with the Holy
Spirit. . . . But you will receive power when the Holy Spirit
comes upon you. And you will be my witnesses, telling people
about me everywhere—in Jerusalem, throughout Judea, in
Samaria, and to the ends of the earth. (Acts 1:1-5, 8)

Acts 2 describes how Jesus's disciples did precisely what He told them to
do. On that day of Pentecost, the Holy Spirit came in power as Christ had
promised. It was evidenced by signs and wonders that drew a crowd of
people who became open and hungry for God's truth. The Holy Spirit's
anointing came upon Peter and the other apostles that day, and they

preached the glorious good news of Jesus with holy boldness. As God's truth was proclaimed in the Holy Spirit's power, three thousand people came to faith in Jesus that day, and His Church was born.

But as with God our Father and with God the Son, continued right relationship with God the Holy Spirit can never be taken for granted and does not automatically remain strong. Haven't we all learned that for any personal relationship to be and stay strong, we must keep making that relationship a personal priority? This requires spending time together and keeping communication open, honest, and real.

I have learned this lesson in my relationship with Helen, my dear wife of nearly fifty years. Because of our covenant of love with one another, we will always be married, and nothing will separate us until death separates us. Though I have taken comfort in this, I have also learned that our relationship can seem distant if I should fail to make our relationship a priority.

It is the same way in the Church's relationship with the Holy Spirit. If we have put our faith and trust in Jesus as Lord and Savior, then we love God because we have confidence that God loves us dearly and know that nothing will ever separate us from His love. God's Word declares it:

> *I am convinced that nothing can ever separate us from God's love. Neither death nor life, neither angels nor demons, neither our fears for today nor our worries about tomorrow—not even the powers of hell can separate us from God's love. No power in the sky above or in the earth below—indeed, nothing in all creation will ever be able to separate us from the love of God that is revealed in Christ Jesus our Lord.* (Romans 8:38-39)

All Christians and local churches can take great comfort in this promise. But we must not ever allow our confidence to lull us into complacency, which could then lead us away from intimacy with God and toward apathy and distance. Because we know that God loves us, and because by His grace we love Him, we are blessed to keep our relationship with God a focused priority in our personal lives and for the local church to which we are called.

This is why the apostle Paul urged the church of Ephesus to continually *be filled with the Holy Spirit* (Ephesians 5:18). This exhortation might be unnecessary if a right relationship with the Holy Spirit automatically happens for His churches. We are to make every effort to seek and depend on the Holy Spirit, thus keeping united with God and one another, for only with the help of the Holy Spirit can such unity be attained. This is why the apostle Paul also urged the church of Ephesus to make every effort toward unity in the Holy Spirit, saying:

> *Therefore I, a prisoner for serving the Lord, beg you to lead a life worthy of your calling, for you have been called by God. Always be humble and gentle. Be patient with each other, making allowance for each other's faults because of your love. Make every effort to keep yourselves united in the Spirit, binding yourselves together with peace. For there is one body and one Spirit, just as you have been called to one glorious hope for the future.* (Ephesians 4:1-4)

What does it look like for a local church to continually *be filled with the Holy Spirit*? What does it mean for the Holy Spirit to lead us *into all truth,* and for us to *know him, because he lives with [us] now and later will be in [us]*? What is required, and what is it like in a local church for the Holy Spirit to *convict the world of its sin, and of God's righteousness, and of the coming judgment*? What does it mean that *the Spirit will tell [us] whatever he receives from [Jesus]*? What does it mean for the church to *be baptized with the Holy Spirit* and to *receive power when the Holy Spirit comes upon [us]*, to *be [Jesus's] witnesses, telling people about [Him] everywhere*?

What does it mean for Christians to keep themselves *united in the Spirit, binding [themselves] together with peace*? What does it mean for our local church that there is *one body and one Spirit,* and that we have *been called to one glorious hope for the future*?

All of these exhortations and promises are addressed by God to the churches. None of these promises has even the remotest possibility of coming to be if we should attempt things in our own strength or by our own volition. But with the Holy Spirit, these are not only possible, but they have been promised and guaranteed. The Holy Spirit has come to be more than Immanuel (God with us), which Jesus, the incarnate Son of God, was in His flesh. The Holy Spirit has come to be God in us.

So what is our part in all of this? We are called and blessed to believe in God the Holy Spirit and to live out this faith. So let's start there. Do you believe, and does your local church believe, in the promise, presence, and power of the Holy Spirit, who is God in us? If you do believe it, your part now is to desire for the Holy Spirit to fill you, guiding you continually, teaching, leading and enabling you for whatever God may have for you to be, do, or say.

As we realize our great need for this gift of the Holy Spirit to be in us, empowering us to follow Jesus, we can hear our heavenly Father inviting us to ask Him. We can come to our Father in faith, asking Him to pour into our hearts more and more of the fullness of the Holy Spirit.

Our motivation in this is not about seeking an experience for ourselves, but in desiring to bring God glory, doing His works and will. The Holy Spirit wants to enable each of us individually, and the church together, for His good purposes. The Holy Spirit therefore brings local churches to a unity that could not be possible without Him.

But for our local churches to have the leading, anointing, and unity that are needed to be who God is calling us to be, and to do the works of Jesus as His body, in His name and with His authority, we must do it in the power and anointing of the Holy Spirit. Biblical local churches will therefore hold firmly to this fundamental faith conviction, depending always on the presence and power of God the Holy Spirit.

For personal reflection: What do you believe, and what has been your experience regarding the person and power of the Holy Spirit, who is God in us? When did you first ask your heavenly Father for the gift of the Holy Spirit, and how consistently are you now seeking to be filled? How is your dependence upon the Holy Spirit affecting your participation in the local church?

For local church leaders' discussion: How has shared faith conviction in the person and power of the Holy Spirit been evident in your leadership team? How could you as church leaders put into practice your dependence upon the Holy Spirit, leading the congregation in desiring and seeking God's will together in biblical unity?

Local Churches Are Connected with Other
Churches in Faith and Mission

As we have seen, the Lord Jesus Christ sees His Church as one – as one whole flock of sheep, or one large extended family. Because of our human limitations, we might have a hard time seeing Christ's Church as He sees it. This difficulty is because we are prone to myopia. Being spiritually nearsighted, we can only see what is close to us. But our Lord's vision is perfect and whole. Seeing all things and all people, God sees His Church as one beautiful bride, one whole and united body.

In John 10 we hear Jesus referring to those who follow Him as His own sheep, and to Himself as our good shepherd: *I am the good shepherd. The good shepherd sacrifices his life for the sheep* (John 10:11). How blessed Jesus's disciples were and are to hear from the Lord that He is and will always be our good shepherd. He will always watch over us, protecting and caring for us. Jesus does this for all who will follow Him!

Now Jesus tells us of His broad perspective from above. Not only does He see and care for the sheep that we see around us, as, for example in our home or local church family, but Jesus sees His entire flock, both Jew and gentile, from every nation, tongue, tribe, and people. This is what He meant when He said, *I have other sheep, too, that are not in this sheepfold. I must bring them also. They will listen to my voice, and there will be one flock with one shepherd* (John 10:16).

Christ's sheepfold is so much larger than the local flock of which we are part. He watches over and cares for His large and scattered people as *one flock with one shepherd.*

We also hear this perspective of Jesus in His High Priestly Prayer:

> *I am praying not only for these disciples but also for all who will ever believe in me through their message. I pray that they will all be one, just as you and I are one—as you are in me, Father, and I am in you. And may they be in us so that the world will believe you sent me. I have given them the glory you gave me, so they may be one as we are one. I am in them, and you are in me. May they experience such perfect unity that the world will know that you sent me and that you love them as much as you love me.* (John 17:20-23)

As Jesus's suffering and death on the cross approached, He prayed from the depths of His soul. His prayer was not only for the disciples who had followed Him throughout His ministry years and who were nearby, but He also prayed *for all who will ever believe in me*. Jesus prayed for His entire global Church *so they may be one as we are one* and so we may *experience such perfect unity that the world will know that you sent me and that you love them as much as you love me*. This prayer was for us.

This was Christ's prayer for His Church and for all of our local churches, because we share His mission now – *that the world may believe that you sent me*. Jesus desires all local churches to truly be connected with other congregations in their shared faith and in the mission He has given us of reaching this world for Him.

As the apostle Paul wrote his letter to the church in Corinth, he also addressed it to *people everywhere who call on the name of our Lord Jesus Christ, their Lord and ours* (1 Corinthians 1:2). Though recognizing the expanse and diversity of our Lord's Church, the apostle reminded the local church in Corinth, and now we are reminded, of our connection with all who call on the name of our Lord Jesus. Paul said it this way: *Some of us are Jews, some are Gentiles, some are slaves, and some are free. But we have all been baptized into one body by one Spirit, and we all share the same Spirit* (1 Corinthians 12:13).

Jesus regards His Church as one extended Church. Yes, we gather in different places and have different personalities, backgrounds, cultures, and customs. We may speak different languages and have many different distinctives. But all true followers of Jesus Christ are bound together as one in Him.

I have experienced this reality firsthand in various congregations across the United States, and in local churches in various countries and cultures. I have seen so many differences in local churches of Jesus Christ, but far above our differences, I have observed the glorious truth that the Church of Jesus Christ is connected as one. Jesus has made us one Church, united together in Him.

The apostle Paul taught this key lesson in his letter to the church of Ephesus: *Make every effort to keep yourselves united in the Spirit, binding yourselves together with peace. For there is one body and one Spirit, just as you have been called to one glorious hope for the future. There is one Lord, one faith, one baptism, one God and Father of all, who is over all, in all, and living through all* (Ephesians 4:3-6).

The clear instruction of this biblical teaching surely applies in our local churches. Within the diversity of our congregation, we are to *make every effort to keep [ourselves] united in the Spirit, binding [ourselves] together with peace.*

A second application of this teaching goes beyond our own local church to the wider body of Christ so that local churches would not see themselves in isolation. We are to seek, see, and participate in the opportunities God gives us to be *united in the Spirit* with other churches, *binding [ourselves] together with peace*. We are to do this because Christ considers and has made His Church to be one, and we should also consider ourselves to be one in Christ.

How grateful and blessed I have been to know and love dear brothers and sisters in Christ from six continents, many islands, and countless nations! How blessed I have been to have led local churches that rightly regarded themselves as part of a worldwide church under Jesus's headship and as connected family with Christians from all nations and many denominations.

In our local churches, the different members are each given gifts by the Holy Spirit. As we come together, with every member contributing and exercising the gifts God has entrusted to them, the local church is able to function effectively as one united church. In the same way, but on a broader scale, our various denominational, regional, or national fellowships of churches, and every local congregation, brings to the collective Church its unique strengths and giftings, thereby blessing, encouraging, and strengthening the wider body of Christ for the building of His Church, and all for the glory of God.

This is why I am so profoundly grateful for the opportunities Christ has afforded me for friendship and ministry with pastors and churches in various circles of connections locally, regionally, nationally, and internationally. All such connections allow us to glorify God by living the miracle of what Christ has done. By conquering the curse of sin through His incarnation and by His death and resurrection, Jesus Christ reconciled unto Himself scattered and divided humanity, and so also reconciles us with one another. Jesus Christ has truly made us one.

Whenever the Church comes together united in the Holy Spirit through common faith in Jesus, we receive shared love and shared mission. We enjoy a foretaste of heaven, being together before the throne of God. As we do so, we anticipate a glorious future day when we will be together before His magnificent majesty:

> *After this I saw a vast crowd, too great to count, from every*
> *nation and tribe and people and language, standing in*
> *front of the throne and before the Lamb. They were clothed*
> *in white robes and held palm branches in their hands. And*
> *they were shouting with a great roar, "Salvation comes*
> *from our God who sits on the throne and from the Lamb!"*
> (Revelation 7:9-10)

What a glorious day it will be when, before God's glorious throne, we will be joined with saints from all the ages, of every generation, tongue, tribe, and people, all giving God praise! Biblical local churches that now experience connection in Jesus Christ with other churches in shared faith and mission locally, nationally, and internationally are blessed now to enjoy this foretaste of heaven.

For personal reflection: Where, when, and how have you experienced connection with other Christians and churches locally, regionally, nationally, or internationally? How does this affect your anticipation of heaven?

For local church leaders' discussion: How has your local church experienced connections with other churches locally, regionally, nationally, or internationally? What could you do to help make this privilege and priority of Jesus even more influential in the life of your church?

Chapter 6

Cautions of Carefulness in Biblical Local Church Governance

Although I have never been a chef, I have encountered some very good ones and have enjoyed the results of their efforts. The finest chefs carefully select the best ingredients, then skillfully utilize them in ways that will achieve an outcome that is pleasing to the ones to whom it is served.

In the previous chapter, we reviewed six essential convictions of biblical leaders and churches that are foundational in Christian living. These could be compared to ingredients in a great recipe. In leading local churches biblically, our aim is to follow Jesus's recipe, doing His will, for His intended outcomes.

Because our shared goal is to make disciples for Jesus as He directs us, we aim to love and lead His church biblically. We will therefore prayerfully and carefully study His Word, aiming to apply it, because we truly long for our local church, which is wholly His, to be everything He intends for it to be.

The six main convictions of biblical churches we considered are key ingredients of our Lord's recipe for biblical churches: (1) God's Word is primary, (2) Jesus Christ is Lord, (3) Jesus is the one and only way to salvation, (4) every local church is under the direct headship of Jesus, (5) local churches depend on the presence and power of God the Holy Spirit, and (6) local churches connect with other churches in faith and mission.

In cooking or baking, have you ever followed a good recipe you thought you knew well, but the outcome wasn't good this time? If so, what did you conclude? Was an essential ingredient omitted, or an insufficient amount used? Were the ingredients applied wrongly? This has happened in our home. In the same way that such lack of carefulness can detrimentally affect results when cooking or baking, much more importantly, it can happen in our local churches. We who are local church leaders must be careful if we want to please our Lord in all that we do.

In this final chapter, our focus will be on four cautions of carefulness that we must carefully apply in local church leadership and governance. These include being careful to live truth like Jesus, to love like Jesus, to pray like Jesus, and to connect like Jesus.

We must carefully ensure that our Lord's "recipe" is being followed for the church to fulfill His purpose. These "cautions of carefulness" are vital for the health of local churches and should not be overlooked, minimized, or ignored, as doing so affects the church's effectiveness. Church leaders are called to continually focus on these aspects in life and ministry.

1. Being Careful to Live the Truth Like Jesus: being wholly focused. This is evidenced in Christ's fulfillment, intimacy, and authority.

We must carefully ensure that the truth of Jesus is our singular focus and that like Him, we are absolutely focused on His truth. We know that our local church lives and ministers in a world filled with lies and deception. We can see the hard consequences of spiritual darkness. But the church is highly privileged to proclaim the one who is the true light of the world (John 8:12). Jesus Christ is the personification of truth. He lived truth, was truth, and is truth. He sets people free from the darkness of deception.

On the evening of His betrayal that would lead to His death, Jesus told His disciples that He was going away and that they would eventually join Him. Hearing this news, His disciples became afraid. They had given up everything to follow Jesus, convinced that He was the Messiah and would soon deliver God's people.

Confused and afraid, Thomas said to Jesus, *We have no idea where you are going, so how can we know the way?* (John 14:5). Condensing the grace of His incarnational life and teaching into one succinct statement, the Lord Jesus answered, *I am the way, the truth, and the life. No one can come to the Father except through me* (John 14:6).

Jesus was telling His disciples then, and He tells His Church now, that He is *the way, the truth, and the life.* At first glance, this claim may sound outrageous. How can Jesus be the only way to God the Father, the ultimate truth and the only giver of everlasting life? His claim was and is astonishing, yet it is entirely true, for Jesus Christ is the personification of truth.

This became the message of the apostles, all of whom were so convinced of it that for the rest of their lives, they were absolutely focused on proclaiming the truth of Jesus, willingly giving their lives to do so. The truth of Jesus has always been the focused message of the Church.

Throughout history, and still today, true followers of Jesus have laid down their lives because of the truth of who Jesus is and what He has accomplished for us. Biblical churches will therefore be absolutely focused on knowing and living the truth of Jesus and faithfully proclaiming it.

John R. W. Stott was a British Anglican priest and theologian who was influential in my formative years of ministry preparation. He was then a leader in the worldwide evangelical movement and he was focused on the basics of historic biblical Christianity. An early book that he authored that greatly blessed me was *Basic Christianity.* It was first published in 1958 by Octavo Press in Cardiff, Wales, United Kingdom, and was republished in 2008 by InterVarsity Press on its fiftieth anniversary. This book was and still remains a classic introduction to true faith in Jesus Christ, the one who has transformed the lives of billions of people, including mine.

In 1974, Stott supervised and coauthored the Lausanne Covenant at the First International World Congress on World Evangelization in Lausanne, Switzerland. Convened by Billy Graham's committee, the congress gathered Christian leaders from 150 nations. It resembled early church councils that united global church leaders in seeking God's guidance. The theme of the congress was "Let the Earth Hear His Voice."

The primary message of the Lausanne Covenant and of John Stott's life, as well as of mine and of all biblical church leaders, is that the truth of Jesus Christ, as revealed in the Bible, is to be believed and proclaimed throughout the world by those who follow Jesus. I was challenged by John Stott's writings and when I was blessed to hear him speak.

In 2005, *Time* magazine listed John R. W. Stott as being among the one hundred most influential people in the world. In the magazine, Billy Graham was quoted as saying this about Stott: "I can't think of anyone who has been more effective in introducing so many people to a biblical world view. He represents a touchstone of authentic biblical scholarship that, in my opinion, has scarcely been paralleled since the days of the 16th-century European Reformers."[21]

In his book *Basic Christianity*, Stott provided a consequential summary of who Jesus Christ is, why we need Jesus Christ, what Jesus Christ has done for us, and how He calls us to respond. I commend this book to you on the theme of the truth of Jesus.

For local churches, I also commend a teaching that was given by Stott at Harvard University in Cambridge, Massachusetts, on March 28, 2012, which can still be heard on YouTube. Stott's lecture was titled "Is Jesus Christ Truth for the 21st Century?"[22] In that lecture he addressed the question of whether Jesus is truly the *veritas* (Latin for "truth") for our time. First he critiqued postmodern relativism, in which truth is considered subjective, so that everyone feels free to determine their own truth. He then observed the absurdity of syncretism, which affirms the validity of all religions as acceptable paths to the same end.

Now, into the darkness of such confusion, the Church comes with the glorious light of truth. We point to Jesus Christ, who declared of Himself, *I am the way, the truth, and the life. No one can come to the Father except through me* (John 14:6).

We and our local churches must consider the question Stott answered that day at Harvard University. We are being challenged by Jesus to consider, answer, and proclaim this answer in our local communities and beyond – concluding that Jesus Christ is indeed the truth for each and all of us here and now, in this place and at this time!

A first caution of carefulness in biblical local church governance is to carefully believe and live the truth of Jesus and, like Jesus, to be absolutely and honestly focused on His truth. This includes being prayerfully sure we are not being tainted by the deceptions of relativism or syncretism.

---

21   *Time* magazine, "Special Issue: The TIME 100," April 10, 2005.

22   John R. W. Stott, "Is Jesus Christ Truth for the 21st Century?" Veritas Forum, Harvard University, March 28, 2012, https://www.youtube.com/watch?v=jddJqWrG3uw.

We must study to ensure that we are standing in faith as God's people upon the unshakeable truths of who Christ is and what He has accomplished for us and for all who believe. Church leaders are to be safeguarding members, ensuring that they are being discipled in the truth of Jesus and that He remains the primary focus and message of the congregation.

In his lecture at Harvard University, Stott used three words to signify and summarize biblical evidence of Jesus still being truth for the twenty-first century. His words were fulfillment, intimacy, and authority. With appreciation and credit to John R. W. Stott, I will briefly review these reflections on the truth of Jesus and suggest applications in this caution of carefulness for local church life and governance.

Fulfillment

Fulfillment is one summary word of the biblical evidence that Jesus is truth. He is not one truth among equal truths, but He is the ultimate fulfillment of truth. In the earliest days of His public ministry, Jesus returned home to Nazareth. One Sabbath day, in the synagogue in Nazareth, where He had grown up, being among people He knew well and who presumed to know Him, Jesus found and read a particular portion from the scroll of Isaiah. The Bible describes what happened:

> *When he came to the village of Nazareth, his boyhood home, he went as usual to the synagogue on the Sabbath and stood up to read the Scriptures. The scroll of Isaiah the prophet was handed to him. He unrolled the scroll and found the place where this was written: "The Spirit of the LORD is upon me, for he has anointed me to bring Good News to the poor. He has sent me to proclaim that captives will be released, that the blind will see, that the oppressed will be set free, and that the time of the Lord's favor has come."*
>
> *He rolled up the scroll, handed it back to the attendant, and sat down. All eyes in the synagogue looked at him intently. Then he began to speak to them. "The Scripture you have just heard has been fulfilled this very day!"* (Luke 4:16-21)

Wow! In His own hometown and among people He had long known and loved, that day Jesus declared the truth that Isaiah's prophecy was about Him. He was announcing that the fulfillment of this prophecy was before them here and now. The townspeople rejected the truth of Jesus that day, even as many do today. But Jesus was and is and forevermore will be the ultimate personification and fulfillment of God's truth.

As time went on, Jesus had more truth to say about Himself that startled many listeners. They rejected and raged at the truth Jesus declared. To people whose identity rested upon their pride in being descendants of Abraham, Jesus spoke startling truth regarding Himself. He said, *Your father Abraham rejoiced as he looked forward to my coming. He saw it and was glad* (John 8:56). Jesus is truth and speaks truth, even when His truth is being rejected.

After rising from the grave, Jesus explained to His disciples that He was the fulfillment of all three sections of the Old Testament, as the Scriptures were divided then. He said He was and is the fulfillment of the law of Moses (Torah) and the Prophets and the Psalms (part of the Wisdom writings of the Bible). Jesus was saying, "All Scripture points to Me." Jesus was declaring to them and to us His truth that He is the fulfillment of God's promise and plan. *He said to them, "These are my words that I spoke to you while I was still with you, that everything written about me in the Law of Moses and the Prophets and the Psalms must be fulfilled"* (Luke 24:44 ESV).

He also said to His disciples, *Blessed are your eyes, because they see; and your ears, because they hear. I tell you the truth, many prophets and righteous people longed to see what you see, but they didn't see it. And they longed to hear what you hear, but they didn't hear it* (Matthew 13:16-17). Jesus was declaring that Abraham, Moses, and all the prophets were living in the age of anticipation, but we who believe in Him now are living in the day of fulfillment. Jesus was telling His disciples then, and is telling us today, that our eyes are seeing, and our ears are hearing, what the Old Testament pillars of faith longed for. This is part of what Jesus meant when He said, *I am . . . the truth.* He was claiming to be more than another prophet. He was and is the fulfillment of prophetic truth.

In Jesus's day, it seemed that everyone was talking about Him. People wondered, and perhaps in some cases argued about, who He could be.

The things He said and did astonished people, but people came to different conclusions about Him. This is undoubtedly true today also. Our human nature often tries to interpret things in ways that can fit in our comfort zone. We find a glimpse of this in Matthew 16, when Jesus asked His disciples, *Who do people say that the Son of Man is?* (Matthew 16:13).

His disciples knew the answer to this because they had heard what people were saying about Him. Some were saying that Jesus was one of the prophets, and some thought He was John the Baptist raised from the dead. Such conclusions were notably wrong. Then Jesus directly asked His disciples the most important question any of us will ever be asked: *But who do you say I am?* (Matthew 16:15). Jesus calls us and our local churches to examine our own hearts, to carefully ensure that we are believing, living, and proclaiming the truth of Jesus Christ.

There are still many people in this world who believe that Jesus was a prophet. Because Muhammed taught this deception in the sixth and seventh centuries AD, Muslims today believe what Muhammed said concerning Jesus – that He was a great historical figure, but only one prophet in a long line of prophets of God. In this denial of the truth of Jesus, Mohammed erroneously claimed and boldly announced regarding himself that he was a prophet of God of greater importance and higher truth than Jesus.

The Bible refers to such deception as the *spirit of the Antichrist* (1 John 4:3). The *spirit of the Antichrist* is in all who deny or oppose the truth of Jesus. As the apostle John was writing *to you who believe in the Son of God* (1 John 5:13), we know that this letter was being circulated among the scattered local churches that were called and desired to proclaim the truth of Jesus. Local church leaders who heard this exhortation were (and are) to prayerfully guard against all deception and to carefully ensure that the truth of Jesus is our focus, and so is being taught, believed, and lived.

In this letter of the apostle John, we read:

> *And who is a liar? Anyone who says that Jesus is not the Christ. Anyone who denies the Father and the Son is an antichrist. Anyone who denies the Son doesn't have the Father, either. But anyone who acknowledges the Son has the Father also.*

*So you must remain faithful to what you have been taught
from the beginning. If you do, you will remain in fellowship
with the Son and with the Father. And in this fellowship we
enjoy the eternal life he promised us.* (1 John 2:22-25)

So Jesus was and is the fulfillment of God's promises. He was and is and forevermore will be *the way, the truth, and the life* (John 14:6).

Applications: How can we apply in local church life and governance this aspect of God's truth – that Jesus Christ is the fulfillment of God's prophetic promises? Consider the following:

1. We can absolutely focus as local church leaders, as members, and as a congregation on knowing Jesus more, and on helping others know Him too. This is to be our goal.

2. We can actively develop opportunities and foster participation for individuals of all ages and levels of spiritual maturity, including nonbelievers and believers at various stages, from new believers to mature believers. This includes children and youth, who can engage in studying, teaching, discussing, and growing in the love and knowledge of Jesus.

Our goal as a local church includes to be continuously learning biblical truths about Jesus, who absolutely fulfills the promises of God.

Intimacy

Intimacy is a second summary word of biblical evidence that Jesus Christ is the truth. Again, Jesus is not one truth among many equal truths. He is the ultimate fulfillment of truth that can bring us into the personal relationships of intimacy with God for which we were created.

Jesus claimed a uniquely intimate relationship with God as His own Father. When just twelve years old, Jesus was already focused on His unique relationship with God, whom He referred to as "My Father." When after three days of searching, Joseph and Mary found their son in the temple, this is what happened:

They finally discovered him in the Temple, sitting among the religious teachers, listening to them and asking questions. All who heard him were amazed at his understanding and his answers. His parents didn't know what to think. "Son," his mother said to him, "why have you done this to us? Your father and I have been frantic, searching for you everywhere."

"But why did you need to search?" he asked. "Didn't you know that I must be in my Father's house? (Luke 2:46-49)

About twenty years later, in the course of His incarnational ministry, Jesus specifically addressed His unique intimacy with God His Father, saying, *My Father has entrusted everything to me. No one truly knows the Son except the Father, and no one truly knows the Father except the Son and those to whom the Son chooses to reveal him* (Matthew 11:27).

Jesus claimed a holy and mutual relationship between Himself and God, His Father. The truth of Jesus includes His intimate and eternal relationship with His Father because Jesus was and is forever God the Son. He is therefore the only one who can lead us into true intimacy with God.

He was addressing our true potential for intimacy with God when He declared, *I am the way, the truth, and the life. No one can come to the Father except through me.* Jesus was saying that He was and is the way to enter into intimacy with God.

Having been forever in intimacy with God the Father, now, in amazing grace and mercy, He has made the way for us to know this intimacy too. This is God's grace to us for the rest of our days and for all eternity. The truth is that Jesus is the way.

He opened the way for our reconciliation and restoration to intimacy with God, for which humanity was created. He took on the judgment of our sin when He hung and died on the cross. By His substitution, our sins were imputed to Jesus, and the relationship He had forever known with God His Father became broken. So when He cried out from the cross, He expressed a deeper agony than the torturous physical pain He was enduring. In the deep despair of broken intimacy, and for the first time in eternity, the Son of God's intimacy with God the Father was broken. It was in the agony of this despair that Jesus, quoting the words of Psalm 22:1, cried out in a loud voice, *"Eli, Eli, lema sabachthani?" which means, "My God, my God, why have you abandoned me?"* (Matthew 27:46).

On the cross, the perfect intimacy between God the Father and the Lord Jesus Christ was broken because of our sin. That is what sin does. It breaks true intimacy. Jesus gave His life to restore for us and all sinful humanity an invitation and opportunity to enter into personal intimacy with God, which is eternal life. This is the glorious message that He gave to His Church to declare in His name.

Jesus, who is the way, the truth, and the life, is the way for all who come in faith to enter in. Jesus said: *You can enter God's Kingdom only through the narrow gate. The highway to hell is broad, and its gate is wide for the many who choose that way. But the gateway to life is very narrow and the road is difficult, and only a few ever find it* (Matthew 7:13-14).

Jesus is the narrow way to everlasting life, which is intimacy with God through faith. This intimacy is for today, for all the days of our life, and for all eternity. He is the way for us to live in intimacy with God now and forevermore. This is the truth of Jesus.

As local church leaders, we are cautioned to carefully ensure that we ourselves are not content to stay at a distance in our relationship with the Lord. In words ascribed to Saint Richard of Chichester, let us pray this prayer: "Thanks be to thee, my Lord Jesus Christ, for all the benefits which thou hast given to me, and for all the pains and insults which thou hast borne for me. O most merciful redeemer, friend, and brother, may I know thee more clearly, love thee more dearly, and follow thee more nearly, day by day."[23]

The last part of St. Richard's prayer of longing for deeper intimacy with the Lord was made popular when I was in my teen years in the musical titled *Godspell* (1971), as these words were adapted for the song "Day by Day." Though I learned this song long ago when in high school, at various times throughout the years I have found myself singing out this prayer to the Lord with longing to "know thee more clearly, love thee more dearly, and follow thee more nearly, day by day."

Church leaders, we are only able to lead a congregation toward

---

23   "The Prayer of St. Richard of Chichester," Generosity Monk, May 16, 2013, https://gener-ositymonk.com/2013/05/16/the-prayer-of-st-richard-of-chichester/.

greater closeness with God to the extent that we ourselves are longing for and enjoying intimacy with Him. This means discipling people in their devotional lives. It means practicing some of the spiritual disciplines, such as Bible reading, Bible study and memorization, generosity, prayer, fasting, and fellowship, to name a few.

Because Jesus is the ultimate truth of the Church, our caution of carefulness is to carefully ensure that the foundation of our shared life, ministry, and governance together as the people of God, and the primary message we proclaim in this world, is focused on the truth of Jesus Christ. It means prioritizing in preaching and teaching and conversation this holy privilege of true intimacy with God through faith in Jesus Christ.

Training for such intimacy with God is very important. When writing to young pastor Timothy, Paul said, *Physical training is good, but training for godliness is much better, promising benefits in this life and in the life to come* (1 Timothy 4:8).

Similarities between physical and spiritual training are informative. Discipline is necessary as the church emphasizes the truth of Jesus, as well as in training ourselves and each other for the outcome of deeper intimacy with God through Jesus. There are a good many things we do in this life that require training in order for us to become good at it. Growing in godliness that leads to deeper intimacy with God requires such training.

Applications: How can the truth of Jesus's intimacy with God the Father be applied in the context of our local church's life and governance? Here are two applications:

1. Because of Jesus's intimacy with God the Father, we can know and celebrate the truth that Christ is indeed our perfect mediator: *There is one God and one Mediator who can reconcile God and humanity—the man Christ Jesus* (1 Timothy 2:5). As local church leaders and as a church family together, in faith we can embrace the promise that because of this truth, we are welcomed now into God's holy presence.

2. In our preaching, teaching, conversations in the church family, and in our daily walk with Jesus, we can know and celebrate the

fact that God is blessing us to live and love in true intimacy with Him. James put it this way: *Come close to God, and God will come close to you* (James 4:8).

Local churches can experience, enjoy, model, and speak about this sweet privilege of being in close personal relationship with God the Father through our Lord Jesus. We are not living or proclaiming arms-length relationships with God. We live and proclaim sweet intimacy with God through Jesus Christ.

Authority

Authority is a third summary word of the biblical evidence that Jesus is truth. The truth of Jesus includes the fact that He has and holds all authority in heaven and on earth. When He was twelve years of age, He astonished the Jewish leaders in Jerusalem by the things He said. Through His years of public ministry, his contemporaries were astonished by the authority with which He spoke. They marveled because the way Jesus spoke was unlike that of the learned scribes who never taught without quoting their authorities.

Jesus did not do that. In His Sermon on the Mount, He said things such as, *You have heard the law that says . . .* , referring to common understandings of Old Testament law; then He said, *but I say . . .* , giving a deeper understanding of God's Word and will (Matthew 5:21-22, 38-39, 43-44). Jesus taught with authority.

He also claimed authority to forgive sins by declaring forgiveness over those who came to Him in humility and faith. When He said to a paralyzed man, *Your sins are forgiven* (Mark 2:5), some teachers of religious law who heard him say this thought, *What is he saying? This is blasphemy! Only God can forgive sins!* (Mark 2:7). They rejected what Jesus said that day, yet He was speaking truth.

Thanks be to God that Jesus has authority to forgive sin. He spoke wonderful words of life to a sinful yet repentant woman who knelt at His feet weeping. He said to her, *Your sins are forgiven* (Luke 7:48). Again, some who heard what He said that day refused to believe that He could do this. They said among themselves, *Who is this man, that he goes around forgiving sins?* (Luke 7:49). Then Jesus said to this woman what He still says today to those who believe in Him and who come to Him in humility and faith: *Your faith has saved you; go in peace* (Luke 7:50).

After His sacrificial death upon the cross and His resurrection in triumphant victory over sin and death, Jesus appeared for forty days at various times and places to His followers. His resurrection appearances were summarized by Paul in his first preserved letter to the local church in Corinth. Paul wrote of the risen Lord Jesus: *He was seen by Peter and then by the Twelve. After that, he was seen by more than 500 of his follow-ers at one time, most of whom are still alive, though some have died. Then he was seen by James and later by all the apostles. Last of all, as though I had been born at the wrong time, I also saw him* (1 Corinthians 15:5-8).

These words are strong evidence of the truth of Paul's testimony because of the very early date of his writing it. Bible scholars almost uniformly affirm that 1 Corinthians was written between AD 51-53, not long after Paul's initial missionary visit to that city that occurred in AD 50-52. Paul remained there for eighteen months sharing the good news of Jesus and establishing that local church. The reference in Acts 18:12 to the governor Gallio helped to ascertain the approximate dates.

In addition, the long list of people who Paul said could testify of hav-ing seen the risen Jesus is also evidence of the truth of the resurrection of Jesus, for he wrote that most of them *are still alive.* As Paul wrote this only about twenty years after Jesus's death, resurrection, and ascension, this shows that the resurrection of Jesus was not a manufactured idea by some delusional or deceptive people.

The truth of Jesus's resurrection is made evident by there being this early in the life of the church hundreds of eyewitnesses who could still be found who would all testify that they had encountered the risen Lord Jesus. Now we are blessed to receive and pass on this glorious truth. Paul wrote, *I passed on to you what was most important and what had also been passed on to me. Christ died for our sins, just as the Scriptures said. He was buried, and he was raised from the dead on the third day, just as the Scriptures said* (1 Corinthians 15:3-4).

This truth of Jesus's resurrection confirms that He lives. And because He lives, He has been given all authority. Jesus addressed this truth just prior to His ascension into heaven. Matthew, who was himself an eyewitness of this event, recorded Jesus's words in the last verses of his gospel: *I have been given all authority in heaven and on earth. Therefore, go and make disciples of all the nations, baptizing them in the name of the Father and the Son and the Holy Spirit. Teach these new disciples to obey all the commands I have given you. And be sure of this: I am with you always, even to the end of the age* (Matthew 28:18-20).

The truth of Jesus Christ is evident in His supreme authority. Of course He is truth, or He could not have forgiven our sins. Of course He is truth, or He could not have risen from the grave. Of course He is truth, or He would not have been given all authority in heaven and on earth, including over the forces of nature, sickness, evil, and the powers of darkness and death and all things.

Applications: What are some applications for your local church life and governance based upon this truth that Jesus Christ has supreme authority? Consider these:

1. Because of Jesus's supreme authority, we who are His Church can know and celebrate the fact that we belong to Jesus. As the Bible says, *You do not belong to yourself, for God bought you with a high price. So you must honor God with your body* (1 Corinthians 6:19-20). As His Church, together we can acknowledge and confess that this life is not our own, for we belong to Jesus Christ. Local church leaders are to lead the way in helping the church acknowledge this truth of Christ's supremacy.

2. Because of Jesus's supreme authority, we who are Christ's Church can know and do His will in all things, which can become our highest goal. In our preaching, teaching, and conversations within the church family, we can be talking about and confessing that Jesus Christ is Lord in our lives and homes, and in His Church.

Because Christ has all authority, our prayerful aim will always be to know and do His will. Our first "caution of carefulness" in local church life is therefore to ensure that we are believing, proclaiming, and aiming to live the truth of Jesus.

For personal reflection: What are some of the personal implications for you of this biblical teaching reality that Jesus Christ is the fulfillment of truth, the way to true intimacy with God, and the one who holds the supreme authority?

For local church leaders' discussion: What does this caution of carefulness mean for you as church leaders, and for your congregation, that you are being called together to carefully proclaim the truth of who Jesus is, being wholly focused on living His truth.

> 2. Being Careful to Love Like Jesus: being sacrificially committed. This is demonstrated in Christ's sacrificial suffering and presence in time.

We are called to carefully ensure that in our local church life, beginning in our own hearts, we are receiving and giving the sacrificial love of Jesus. We are to carefully ensure that our primary focus is not on physical property or on acquiring, accomplishing, or doing things that will not endure. Rather, we are called to ensure that all we do is in love, and that we are loving sacrificially like Jesus.

Have you ever contemplated why you were given this gift of life? Or on a broader scale, why was humanity put on this planet? One of the primary reasons is love. God put us here to be loved and to love. We must not miss this important truth.

God created us because of His great love, so we might receive it, return it, and give it to others in Jesus's name. God created us for love. Too easily the people of God may wrongly conclude that we were chosen and saved because of some merit of our own or some good thing we have done. We might arrogantly presume that we are better or more deserving than others. This is spiritual pride.

Perhaps we are clinging tightly to our known sins, to the hurt we have caused others, or to the shame we feel because of our failures, and so we have wrongly concluded that we are unloved or unworthy to be loved. To all the self-righteous and the self-doubting, God tells us of His very great love for us. In a time of hard circumstances, God said this to His people through His servant Moses:

The LORD did not set his heart on you and choose you
because you were more numerous than other nations, for
you were the smallest of all nations! Rather, it was simply
that the LORD loves you, and he was keeping the oath he
had sworn to your ancestors. That is why the LORD rescued
you with such a strong hand from your slavery and from
the oppressive hand of Pharaoh, king of Egypt. Understand,
therefore, that the LORD your God is indeed God. He is the
faithful God who keeps his covenant for a thousand genera-
tions and lavishes his unfailing love on those who love him
and obey his commands. (Deuteronomy 7:7-9)

God was saying then and is still saying now, "I love you because I love you."

In the New Testament, God reinforced this truth as the reason Jesus Christ came to give His life for sinners. He did it because of God's great love. The apostle Paul put it this way in his letter addressed to the church in Rome: *When we were utterly helpless, Christ came at just the right time and died for us sinners. Now, most people would not be willing to die for an upright person, though someone might perhaps be willing to die for a person who is especially good. But God showed his great love for us by sending Christ to die for us while we were still sinners* (Romans 5:6-8).

The apostle John stated it this way in his gospel: *For this is how God loved the world: He gave his one and only Son, so that everyone who believes in him will not perish but have eternal life. God sent his Son into the world not to judge the world, but to save the world through him* (John 3:16-17). God was saying then, and is saying to us now, "I love you because I love you." All local churches are called to accept and celebrate this truth of God's great love for us. This is to be our confidence, hope, and message. God's love is the ultimate reason we live – to receive God's love by faith, to return God's love in a lifestyle of worship, and to give God's love to others in Jesus's name.

This caution of carefulness in biblical local church governance is to carefully ensure that we are loving sacrificially like Jesus. We know this is very important because the Bible makes it clear that Jesus said so.

I hope you know it is okay and very good to ask questions of God, seeking to understand and know His truth. But I have learned, and I know well, that because God is infinite in wisdom and knowledge, and because I am finite and limited in understanding, I cannot possibly comprehend all of God's truth or why God does all He does. But the Bible has promised, and I have experienced the truth of His Word.

The Bible invites us with God's amazing promises such as *Keep on seeking, and you will find* (Matthew 7:7), and *Come close to God, and God will come close to you* (James 4:8). Although we cannot possibly understand all of God's ways, I have experienced the truth of God's promises. If we seek God in faith, God meets us, revealing the truth of His great love for us.

As for understanding the importance of love in all that we do as followers of Jesus and as local churches, this revelation only comes to those who are seeking God and His truth. Mark 12 tells of the time when a teacher of religious law approached Jesus with a question that flowed from his lifetime of seeking to know and please God. He had studied God's law because he wanted to obey God. Jesus's answer to his question spoke to that religious man in his day, and it speaks to followers of Jesus and local churches in our day:

> One of the teachers of religious law was standing there listening to the debate. He realized that Jesus had answered well, so he asked, "Of all the commandments, which is the most important?"
>
> Jesus replied, "The most important commandment is this: 'Listen, O Israel! The LORD our God is the one and only LORD. And you must love the LORD your God with all your heart, all your soul, all your mind, and all your strength.' The second is equally important: 'Love your neighbor as yourself.' No other commandment is greater than these."
>
> The teacher of religious law replied, "Well said, Teacher. You have spoken the truth by saying that there is only one God and no other. And I know it is important to love him with all my heart and all my understanding and all my strength, and to love my neighbor as myself. This is more important than to offer all of the burnt offerings and sacrifices required in the law." (Mark 12:28-33)

Jesus said that the most important commandment of all is to love God with all that we are and have. He said that the second most important commandment is to love our neighbors as ourselves. Jesus was saying and still says that the most important priority in Christian discipleship is to love God and love others. Church leaders are to carefully ensure that love is our motivation and message in who we are and all that we do personally, as leaders, and as a local church of God's people.

Jesus emphasized this message over and over again. In John 13, He took us deeper in our understanding of this commandment. After telling His disciples about His imminent suffering and death, and after lovingly and humbly washing their filthy feet, Jesus said this about what He desires for His disciples to do now with His love: *Now I am giving you a new commandment: Love each other. Just as I have loved you, you should love each other. Your love for one another will prove to the world that you are my disciples* (John 13:34-35).

Jesus makes it clear that we who have received His love are now to prioritize loving others like Jesus has loved us. In the local church, we must carefully ensure that this is always our focus and priority.

Let's think about this personally first, then collectively, because local churches are comprised of individual members who come together in Jesus's name. We can start by encouraging one another to personally receive His love and extend it to others. How can we do this? Every morning as we wake up, we can choose to immediately fix our focus on Jesus, making a faith decision that today we will prioritize love.

I know something about depression, for at times I have fought that battle. And as a pastor and Navy Chaplain, I have counseled many who fight it too. Sometimes at the end of the day, especially when trials, struggles, or disappointments come, we might fix our focus there, concluding, "I failed today." Whenever something goes wrong and the burdens become heavier, this might become our standard response. When this is so, it is no wonder if a cloud of hopelessness or depression should settle upon us.

I suggest a better way, which is God's way for His children. Let us carefully fix our focus upon Jesus Christ, making a faith decision today and every day to prioritize love. We can start by choosing to believe and receive God's love for us. When this happens, we discover the sweet truth that God's love is constant, consistent, and steady, and that nothing can ever separate us from it. This is biblical truth for today:

> *I am convinced that nothing can ever separate us from God's love. Neither death nor life, neither angels nor demons, neither our fears for today nor our worries about tomorrow— not even the powers of hell can separate us from God's love. No power in the sky above or in the earth below—indeed, nothing in all creation will ever be able to separate us from the love of God that is revealed in Christ Jesus our Lord.* (Romans 8:38-39)

Despite our sinfulness and tendency to wander, God's love keeps drawing us back. In a world in which giving and receiving love is often conditional and fleeting, God's love is stable, healing, comforting, and a source of refuge. Though we may not always feel like God loves us, His love for us is continuous and unconditional.

A Morning Devotion on the Love of God

All my life I've been blessed to start the day with a spiritual breakfast of God's Word, worship, and prayer. God meets me, feeds me, and strengthens me for the day that is ahead. Why would you or I ever choose to miss out on such an available blessing?

With this image in mind, here is a "favorite breakfast" that I highly recommend. I hope that like me, you may enjoy this breakfast of God's love as part of your own daily diet. It is very good for God's children to read, meditate, worship, intercede, and thank God for His faithfulness and promises each day, in faith seeing yourself as a recipient of God's promise. Enjoy this spiritual breakfast with the Lord:

1. Read God's Word. For example, read the following promises concerning God's love. Whenever God teaches you and wherever you see a promise of God, insert yourself into the teaching and add your own name into the promise, as God speaks this to you.

Concerning the promise of God's great love for you and for us all:

For this is how God loved the world: He gave his one and only Son, so that everyone who believes in him will not perish but have eternal life. (John 3:16)

But God showed his great love for us by sending Christ to die for us while we were still sinners. (Romans 5:8)

Give all your worries and cares to God, for he cares about you. (1 Peter 5:7)

No power in the sky above or in the earth below—indeed, nothing in all creation will ever be able to separate us from the love of God that is revealed in Christ Jesus our Lord. (Romans 8:39)

2. Meditate on God's Word. Ponder and enjoy in faith what God has spoken to you today. Don't rush from the table. Savor what God has fed you. Enjoy again the truth that God loves you so much. Let this strengthen you for today.

3. Worship and praise – loving God back. This is the greatest commandment. Worship by loving the one who first loved you. Tell God what He means to you and how you are indebted to Him for saving you by His grace. Take time to love God.

4. Intercede for the burdens and people on your heart. In a faith-filled response, ask God for help accepting His invitation to *give all your worries and cares to God, for he cares about you* (1 Peter 5:7). As you pray, be prayerfully available to love God by loving others, asking God to lay upon your own mind and heart anyone to whom He would have you reach out with His love today.

5. Thank God again for His grace to you, and be grateful for every blessing, especially for your eternal salvation in Christ Jesus. Read and reflect again on this truth concerning you: *God saved you by his grace when you believed. And you can't take credit for this; it is a gift from God. Salvation is not a reward for the good things*

we have done, so none of us can boast about it (Ephesians 2:8-9). Reflect with gratitude on this assurance that God's gift of grace in saving you was not because of anything you did or accomplished, but it was by God's grace through your faith in Jesus Christ. This grace was prompted by His love for you.

At the start and end of every day, and in all moments in between, we can rest in God's great love for us. Because God's first priority is love, the church's must be too. And this speaks to the local church.

The church's primary focus must not be on projects or activities that offer temporary enjoyment or comfort. Our focus must not be on a property or building for purposes of earthly ease or esthetic beauty. Should these become our focus, we will miss out on opportunities that God has prepared for us to receive and enjoy His love, or for us to bring His love to others in Jesus's name.

Each of us individually and all of us collectively in the local church are to take the time to prayerfully receive and reflect on God's love, and to give His love in Jesus's name. The Bible exhorts us to *do everything with love* (1 Corinthians 16:14).

When love becomes our highest priority as a church, we will be more focused on personal relationships than on personal accomplishments. God's call for churches is to show His love in relationships with others. This is beautifully seen in 1 Corinthians 13. This is how God loves us, and it is how God enables us to love others in the name of Jesus.

> *Love is patient and kind. Love is not jealous or boast-*
> *ful or proud or rude. It does not demand its own way. It is*
> *not irritable, and it keeps no record of being wronged. It*
> *does not rejoice about injustice but rejoices whenever the*
> *truth wins out. Love never gives up, never loses faith, is*
> *always hopeful, and endures through every circumstance.*
> (1 Corinthians 13:4-7)

God loves us like this; and because of God's love for us, He is patient with us. Knowing our human frailties, God is kind. God is not envious, boastful, or easily angry. And contrary to the imaginations of so many Christians, God does not keep a record of our wrongs, because in Jesus Christ we are fully forgiven. God always protects us. Elsewhere and in a season of trial for God's people, we hear God saying, *"I know the plans I have for you," says the* LORD. *"They are plans for good and not for disaster, to give you a future and a hope"* (Jeremiah 29:11).

God always perseveres and never ever fails. This is how God loves us, and it is how God enables us to be loving in His name, even to love those who may seem to us to be unloving or unlovable. God loves us even when we fail and fall, and He enables His churches to do the same.

What does it look like for a local church to love as God loves us? There are many ways to answer this question, but we will focus on the sacrifices of our commitment and of our time.

Loving Like Jesus Includes the Sacrifice of Commitment

We cannot love like Jesus without making a sacrifice of commitment. I contemplate this every year in the season of the church calendar called Lent. As "Holy Week" approaches and proceeds, Christians reflect on the depth of Christ's love for us, and of all He accomplished for us by His sacrifice of love.

Jesus's suffering and sacrificial death, giving Himself to the abuse of mockery, scourging, and death by crucifixion, was motivated by the deep, deep love of God. The Bible says that all of this took place because of the love of God.

> *This is how God loved the world: He gave his one and only Son, so that everyone who believes in him will not perish but have eternal life.* (John 3:16)

> *This is my commandment: Love each other in the same way I have loved you. There is no greater love than to lay down one's life for one's friends.* (John 15:12-13)

> *When we were utterly helpless, Christ came at just the right time and died for us sinners. Now, most people would not be willing to die for an upright person, though someone might*

perhaps be willing to die for a person who is especially good. But God showed his great love for us by sending Christ to die for us while we were still sinners. And since we have been made right in God's sight by the blood of Christ, he will certainly save us from God's condemnation. For since our friendship with God was restored by the death of his Son while we were still his enemies, we will certainly be saved through the life of his Son. So now we can rejoice in our wonderful new relationship with God because our Lord Jesus Christ has made us friends of God. (Romans 5:6-11)

We know how much God loves us, and we have put our trust in his love. God is love, and all who live in love live in God, and God lives in them. And as we live in God, our love grows more perfect. So we will not be afraid on the day of judgment, but we can face him with confidence because we live like Jesus here in this world. Such love has no fear, because perfect love expels all fear. If we are afraid, it is for fear of punishment, and this shows that we have not fully experienced his perfect love. We love each other because he loved us first. (1 John 4:16-19)

This is how much God loves us. And because Christ's Church is so deeply loved like this, our local churches can love like this by and through our sacrificial commitments in Jesus's name. One primary relationship where this applies is marriage. The love of sacrificial commitment also applies in all family relationships, including in personal relationships of the local church, which is the family of God.

Throughout the years of my marriage, I've often been challenged by reading the following verses and then contemplating the depth of Christ's sacrificial love for the Church and for me. I've then asked God to help me love Helen with the sacrificial commitment described: *Husbands, . . . love your wives, just as Christ loved the church. He gave up his life for her to make her holy and clean, washed by the cleansing of God's word* (Ephesians 5:25-26).

Loving someone with this kind of sacrificial commitment means willingly giving of oneself to the other, even if it costs us, and even when it costs us dearly. Loving someone with sacrificial commitment means not quitting that relationship but willingly forgiving and doing whatever it takes to lovingly reconcile when a relationship has become broken. This is loving like Jesus. Strong marriages and healthy churches reflect Jesus's love like that.

Loving Like Jesus Includes the Sacrificing of Time

Loving like Jesus requires going and giving of our time to be with people in their need where they are. In military chaplaincy, we called this "ministry of presence." This is what Jesus Christ did for us. The Son of God loved us so much that He willingly left the glory of heaven to enter our space and time to be Immanuel, God with us. This is the glory of His incarnation as it was prophesied by Isaiah, celebrated by Matthew, and described by John:

> *The Lord himself will give you the sign. Look! The virgin will conceive a child! She will give birth to a son and will call him Immanuel (which means "God is with us").* (Isaiah 7:14, quoted in Matthew 1:23)

> *The Word became flesh and dwelt among us, and we have seen his glory, glory as of the only Son from the Father, full of grace and truth.* (John 1:14 ESV)

This does not imply that the Word that became flesh ceased being God. Rather, it means that the Word, who was God, decisively entered humanity by taking upon Himself human flesh and nature. This is the most amazing event of human history.

Motivated by infinite and eternal love, the Creator of all things, the everlasting, omniscient, omnipotent, and omnipresent God, chose to be God with us, entering into the limits of time and humanity. The apostle Paul urged the local church in Philippi to consider this amazing example of Jesus and to live and love like that. He said:

You must have the same attitude that Christ Jesus had.
Though he was God, he did not think of equality with God as
something to cling to. Instead, he gave up his divine privi-
leges; he took the humble position of a slave and was born
as a human being. When he appeared in human form, he
humbled himself in obedience to God and died a criminal's
death on a cross. (Philippians 2:5-8)

Loving like Jesus requires sacrificing time. Ponder for a moment the gift the Son of God made when *he gave up his divine privileges*, not being born into luxury, but taking *the humble position of a slave* and being *born as a human being*. Consider His sacrifice for us and ask God to help you love like that. Pray this for your local church, that in humility you might give of yourselves in the sacrifice of being present in time.

This only happens to the extent that we have first made a commitment to be with God, making it our way of life to be with Him. Spending time with God means having a personal and collective agenda to enjoy His presence, listen and commune with God, and leaning on Him in faith and love.

This is to be our personal discipline of setting aside daily quiet time to be with God. Loving people like Jesus loves us means doing what Jesus did, taking time and giving time to be with people out of love.

Over the years, I have been blessed to have participated in hundreds of funerals and celebrations of life. During such times, stories are told, and testimonies are shared about the life that was lived by the one who has died. I've never heard anyone say something like, "This person was so good at getting everything done on his to-do list," or "It was beautiful to see how this person was always so busy." I have never heard that.

Numerous testimonials have affirmed the significant impact of spending time together, emphasizing that one's presence can be the most valuable gift one can offer. During such moments, transformative experiences may occur. Followers of Jesus are encouraged to emulate His love by dedicating their time and presence selflessly to those whom God calls them to love and serve.

Even when, humanly speaking, Jesus had good reasons not to give His time right then, He still showed compassionate love, pausing whatever He was doing to give attention and time. For example, after being notified of the death of John the Baptist, whom He dearly loved, notice what Jesus did: *As soon as Jesus heard the news, he left in a boat to a remote area to be alone. But the crowds heard where he was headed and followed on foot from many towns. Jesus saw the huge crowd as he stepped from the boat, and he had compassion on them and healed their sick* (Matthew 14:13-14).

While intending to have some time alone, Jesus encountered people in need, *had compassion on them*, and gave them His presence and time. Often when Jesus did this, it was in the midst of pressing personal demands. If we find ourselves too busy to offer presence and time to others due to our numerous commitments, it can be helpful to prayerfully consider Jesus's example and follow Him. When it seemed like everyone clamored for Jesus's attention, He saw and responded to divine appointments. With deep love, Jesus sacrificially offered Himself.

We have all been there at times, haven't we – when we've been completely focused on our long to-do list? At such times, we might not even notice the people around us whom God has brought across our path for His divine purposes. But if we truly want to be like Jesus, and if we pray toward this end, He will answer this prayer.

It can be helpful for the church to read and prayerfully study some biblical examples of Jesus pausing along the way and giving His presence and time with His heart of love. Here are ten biblical examples of Jesus doing this (and there are many more that could be given). Let each of us who desire to follow Jesus (and let the churches together read and consider these) ask the Holy Spirit to teach us more about the love of Jesus demonstrated here:

1. Bartimaeus (Mark 10:46-52)

2. Jairus (Mark 5:21-43)

3. The woman with a bleeding problem (Mark 5:32-34)

4. Zacchaeus (Luke 19:1-10)

5. The little children (Mark 10:13-16)

6. The woman at the well (John 4:1-42)

7. The immoral woman at the Pharisee's party (Luke 7:36-50)

8. The man with a legion of demons (Mark 5:1-20)

9. Two blind men (Matthew 20:30-34)

10. The women weeping as He carried His cross (Luke 23:28-31)

Then let us pray: "Dear Jesus, help me to sacrificially love like You. Lord, help us as Your church to sacrificially love like You. Help us to sacrificially give of ourselves, of our presence, and of our time in Your great name, and for Your praise and glory. Amen."

Over and over again, we see Jesus pausing from whatever He was doing or wherever He was going to take time for people. This meant recognizing and responding to the divine appointments that were prepared for Him. In His humanity, Jesus could not address every need of every person in the places He ministered. Of necessity, Jesus experienced limitations.

To take upon Himself the limits of human nature and flesh, the Son of God was required to lay aside for a while certain prerogatives of His divinity. These included the fullest expressions of His divine omniscience, omnipotence, and omnipresence. Like all humanity, Jesus faced limited time, strength, and availability. He too became dependent upon prayer and the anointing and empowering of the Holy Spirit.

Jesus's life of prayer and the anointing of the Holy Spirit equipped Him to recognize and respond to divine appointments such as Zachaeus in the tree, Bartimaeus along the roadside in Jericho, and the outcast woman at the well in Sychar. Jesus sacrificially invested time and presence in people – and praise God, He still does!

Aren't you glad that the Bible is wholly true, including the sweet promise of Hebrews 13:8, that *Jesus Christ is the same yesterday, today, and forever*? Jesus is the same today as He was then. This means He has time and will be present with you and will give attention to you whenever you approach Him in faith. With compassionate love, He meets us in our need – every single time. This has been my life experience.

Being intentionally careful to love like Jesus loves includes sacrificially giving to people the gift of our availability and time. Yes, we must be wise about it, because we do have limited time and strength, but following the beautiful example of Jesus Christ will include having unselfish willingness to lovingly give of our availability and time. This is the Lord's call to His Church, and to each of our local churches.

This poem is my own prayer of availability. I prayerfully hope to give the gift of presence and time that Jesus Christ has given to me.

"The Sweet Gift of Time"

Lord, I thank You for this sweet gift of time,
time You have given to me.

As You have given it, let me give too,
for it is You who I want them to see.

In Jesus's name, Lord, help me to gladly give
my presence in time,

So your purposes will be fulfilled,
reflecting love divine.

Help me give time to listen and time to pray,
time to help and time to say,

Time to stay or time to go,
time to reap and time to sow;

Time for labor and time for fun,
time for groups and time for one.

I give to You my time today.
It is all for You, dear Lord, I pray.

How can we invest time as Jesus did? We can start by thinking of the relationships that matter most to us: spouse, children, sweetheart, family relationships, neighbors, coworkers, or friends. At the end of each day, and at the end of our lives, we will not regret having taken time for what matters most to us. Let us thus be making room and taking time to be present for showing Christ's love and our love by being present and giving the gift of our time.

And because God knows and loves us, including people you love and people you do not yet know, but whom He will bring across your path, God wants to use you and the people of your local church to tangibly love those whom God loves and for whom Jesus died. Jesus wants His Church and every local church to be His hands and feet, His voice and heart, His compassionate love. This requires our sacrificial availability and time.

The Bible reminds us of the brevity of this life and how our days pass by so quickly, like grass and flowers. The Lord declared this through the prophet Isaiah: *Shout that people are like the grass. Their beauty fades as quickly as the flowers in a field. The grass withers and the flowers fade beneath the breath of the* LORD. *And so it is with people. The grass withers and the flowers fade, but the word of our God stands forever* (Isaiah 40:6-8).

Billy Graham's last book, which he wrote when approaching his ninety-third birthday, has blessed me greatly, as I too am aging. I have often been reminded that indeed, life withers and fades. In his book, *Nearing Home: Life, Faith, and Finishing Well*,[24] Graham addressed the shortness of life and our biblical challenge of making each day count for God until our last breath.

All of us have a finite number of days, but none of us knows how many remain. But through faith in Jesus, we are able to live every remaining day in a personal relationship with God, being inspired daily by God's timeless Word that stands firm forever, and we can devote our time in available service to the one whose love endures forever.

Concerning this caution of carefulness to ensure that our local church is indeed loving like Jesus, how does this affect the way He leads us, and how we are governed? It means that like Him, we will make noticeable and sacrificial commitments in ministry, and we will invest our availability and time to care for one another, giving help when it's needed within the congregation.

It also means that as a church family, we will take proactive and observable initiatives in our local community to address real needs. We will do this through the gifts of resources God has entrusted to us, including our availability and time.

---

24 Billy Graham, *Nearing Home: Life, Faith, and Finishing Well* (Nashville: W Publishing Group, a trademark of Thomas Nelson, 2011)

Carefully confirming that the local church loves like Jesus includes prayerfully ensuring that in decision-making, budget setting, and calendar planning, our focus is not only or not even primarily on what we prefer, desire, or need. Our Lord wants us to be outward focused, having His heart for people who are lost, lonely, and hurting.

Local churches that love like Jesus loves will aim to prayerfully discern the very real needs of people who are around them, and whom God dearly loves. It will mean asking the Holy Spirit to lead us in demonstrating His love in practical and noticeable ways. This will require sacrificial commitment in Jesus's name and prioritizing the compassionate and sacrificial generosity of our time.

Such expressions of love in and by local churches require us to realize that we are stewards rather than owners. If, for example, God has blessed us with facilities or with financial resources, we know we are not owners of them, but are stewards of what is God's, so we gladly share what is His as a blessing to the community and to the world. This concept of stewardship also applies to our strength and to our time.

As the local church shares our Lord's resources by our loving ministry of presence, in grace God will bring some people to notice and inquire, "Why are you doing this?" The church can then testify that it is because of the love of God in Jesus Christ.

Mike Chong Perkinson, in his honest book *Radically Living, Quietly Dying*, gives powerful insights into hidden pain and the way out that God so lovingly provides. He says that what Jesus has done for us is now the Church's model for ministry: "Jesus came and lived among us, pitched His tent as one of us, walked with His flawed and passionate disciples, and revealed to us who the Father is and what a Son truly looks like walking in a relationship with the Father. We are not the incarnation, but surely we can live incarnationally as we were created from relationship for relationship (Genesis 1:26-28). So give the gift of presence!"[25] This is what local churches do as they carefully aim to love like Jesus.

Applications: What are some applications for your local church life and governance in aiming to love like Jesus? Consider these:

25 Mike Chong Perkinson, *Radically Living, Quietly Dying* (Indianapolis: Light and Life Publishing, 2024), 236.

1. We can train, disciple, encourage, and help each other enjoy a daily diet of the love of God by reading, meditating, believing, and thanking God for His love for us.

2. We can preach, teach, disciple, and talk with one another within our church family about God's great love, affirming and celebrating sacrificial commitments, and giving of ourselves personally and as a congregation in Jesus's name, even when it costs us.

3. We can aim to budget as stewards of what is God's, giving of church resources, including our presence and time in Jesus's name, wherever God may lead us.

To review, a first caution of carefulness we considered in local church life and governance is carefully ensuring that we are believing, proclaiming, and living the truth of Jesus. A second caution of carefulness we have considered in local church governance is to carefully ensure that we are sacrificially committed to give of ourselves in Jesus's name. This means giving of God's resources, including our time to love like Jesus.

For personal reflection: What are personal implications of Christ's calling you to love others as He has loved you? In what ways have you been loving sacrificially? For whom might Jesus be calling you to love now through a gift of time?

For local church leaders' discussion: What does this caution of carefulness mean for you as church leaders, and for your church family together, as you are called by Jesus to ensure that you are loving sacrificially, as He has loved you?

> 3. Being Careful to Pray Like Jesus: prioritizing and
> practicing prayer. This is taught in Christ's lifestyle
> of prayer and in how He taught us to pray.

We must carefully ensure that we are praying as a way of life in the Church – never as an afterthought, but always as a main thought. As local churches we are blessed to pray to God the Father through Jesus Christ. We are to pray like Jesus, for Jesus, and always in Jesus's name!

Why does the church need to be reminded to be careful about prioritizing and practicing prayer like Jesus? It is because history has shown, and our own experience has confirmed, that churches are too prone to minimize prayer, presuming that we can proceed in our own strength and wisdom. Praying like Jesus prayed and as He taught us increases our faith, strengthens us in the power of God, and opens doors for the move of God, all for His glory and praise.

In the fourth chapter of this book, when considering biblical principles, the important principle was emphasized that local church members are to be living under Jesus's headship. This requires church members to be praying like Jesus, as He taught us to pray.

My emphasis here on certain cautions of carefulness for churches includes that local church leaders are to be carefully ensuring that a lifestyle of prayer is happening in the local church. This will mean scheduling, structuring, prioritizing, and practicing prayer as our way of life in the church. It will be more than something we talk about; it will be something we cannot live without.

Of course, this can and will only happen to the extent that local church leaders and members are themselves prioritizing and practicing prayer. Leaders will bathe in prayer all that they do. Every decision that is to be made will flow from prayers of trust and dependence upon God. Praying like this in the local church does not automatically happen, but we can be careful to ensure that it does happen.

The apostle Paul, who established, loved, and visited many local churches, urged the churches to prioritize prayer – as, for example, this exhortation in his letter to the church in Colossae: *Devote yourselves to prayer with an alert mind and a thankful heart* (Colossians 4:2). What does this mean for us and for local churches?

Several times in the Gospels, we find Jesus teaching on this theme. One such occasion was in His powerful Sermon on the Mount when Jesus taught us this: *Keep on asking, and you will receive what you ask for. Keep on seeking, and you will find. Keep on knocking, and the door will be opened to you. For everyone who asks, receives. Everyone who seeks, finds. And to everyone who knocks, the door will be opened* (Matthew 7:7-8).

Notice again Jesus's promise to us. He promises to each of us, and to all of our local churches, that *everyone who asks, receives.* Doesn't that sound like a promise that you personally, and your local church together, would be foolish to ignore and wise and blessed to believe and do? This promise of the Lord Jesus is for everyone who asks. Let us be very careful, then, to ensure that we are in fact prioritizing and practicing prayer as Jesus taught us.

Jesus tells us what it means to be a praying church. It means asking, seeking, knocking, and speaking with God about whatever is occurring, about the decisions we would make in God's will and for God's glory, and about circumstances that need a touch of God's grace and power. Let's now flesh out a little more about these biblical terms.

Ask: Jesus said, *Keep on asking, and you will receive what you ask for* (Matthew 7:7). He taught us that to ask of God is to persistently pray. *Jesus told his disciples a story to show that they should always pray and never give up* (Luke 18:1). Local church leaders who desire to be biblical in their church governance must carefully ensure that their members are being discipled in practicing persistent prayer, and that they do so themselves. This requires a lifestyle of prayer personally, as church leaders together, and as a local church.

Seek: Jesus said, *Keep on seeking, and you will find* (Matthew 7:7). He calls us to seek Him above all – not occasionally, but to always *keep on seeking.* God has promised that when we do, we will surely find Him, and we will know His will. *If you look for me wholeheartedly, you will find me* (Jeremiah 29:13).

Earlier in His Sermon on the Mount, Jesus said this about our seeking: *Seek first the kingdom of God and his righteousness, and all these things will be added to you* (Matthew 6:33 esv). Local church leaders who want to be biblical in local church governance will carefully ensure that in their own hearts, in their leadership, and in what they model and teach the congregation, they are fixing their own eyes upon Jesus, seeking Him above all else.

Our Lord calls His churches to not presume that we have already learned what we need to know or have already gained what He intends for us. Instead, with increasing thirst and hunger in our hearts for deeper intimacy with Jesus, we will guide His Church to do what we will do – to *keep on seeking*.

We must remind ourselves and each other of the blessing of seeking God daily. Seeking God continually is the foundation for spiritual growth. It is more than simply having a devotional life that includes prayer and reading the Bible. Seeking God continually includes longing for God's presence to change us for His purpose and glory. Biblical church governance includes sharing a longing for more of Jesus and seeking Him in all we do. Leaders are to carefully ensure that they are personally seeking Jesus first, and that the church they lead and are part of continually seeks Jesus too.

Knock: Jesus said, *Keep on knocking, and the door will be opened to you* (Matthew 7:7). He promises that when we knock on His door, He will hear and open the door. Let's reflect on this image for a moment. Why do people knock on a door? We knock because we want to come in, or we want to talk with the person on the other side of that door. Of course, sometimes the one we want to talk with is not available.

Have you ever experienced, as I have, the frustration of knocking on a door when you knew that the person you were looking for was in fact on the other side of that door, but no one answered, and the door stayed unopened. That can be painful, can't it?

But Jesus promises His church that when we *keep on knocking*, He opens the door. What a beautiful promise this is! Do you want to meet with Jesus and talk with Him? You can knock on His door, and He will invite you in. You can talk with Jesus.

I heard a children's devotional on this biblical theme that was given at a local church. Because children can think concretely, a question was raised about where the door is located, or "What is God's address?" A good answer given was "the Bible," for there God meets us and speaks. As we pray, speaking with God about anything on our hearts, He opens the door for us to hear and answer our prayers.

Another question raised was "Why doesn't God immediately answer?"

Again, Jesus tells us to *keep on knocking.* He wants us to patiently trust Him, believing in faith that He is going to give an answer; so we keep on knocking.

Whenever someone has invited you over and you know they are home, do you leave if they don't immediately answer the door? Of course not! You keep on knocking, don't you? And you wait patiently until the door is opened.

Knocking continually is about persistence in our desire for close fellowship with God. It is believing that God hears and will surely answer according to His will and in His time. Biblical church governance requires praying with persistence about everything, knowing that the church needs the mind of Christ, and believing in faith that He is surely going to answer.

Leaders are cautioned to carefully ensure that they are personally knocking with persistence for the burdens that are on their own hearts, and that they are leading the church in doing the same. This includes thanking Jesus for the doors that are opened for us, and for the blessed opportunity we have to keep knocking on His door, believing and waiting in faith for promised answers.

Speak: Jesus gives His church a wonderful promise that comes to us through His invitation to bring to Him and speak with Him about every situation and burden. He said, *For everyone who asks, receives. Everyone who seeks, finds. And to everyone who knocks, the door will be opened.*

Jesus calls His church to ask, seek, and knock. But to whom? He calls His churches to speak with Him about all of their life and ministry together.

Applications: What are some applications for your local church life and governance in aiming to pray like Jesus? Consider the following:

1. We can train, disciple, encourage, and help one another to live a lifestyle of prayer in dependence on God, ensuring that we have many opportunities to pray together.

2. In preaching, teaching, discipling, and conversing with one another in the church family, we can aim to teach and live in a culture of persistent prayer and dependence on God as Jesus invited us to

do in Matthew 7:7-8 – to continually ask, seek, knock, and speak in faith to our Lord, as our way of life together.

For personal reflection: What are personal implications of God's invitation and calling for you to pray like Jesus? In what ways have you been asking, seeking, knocking, and speaking in persistent prayer as Christ has taught us?

For local church leaders' discussion: What does this caution of carefulness mean for you as church leaders, and for your church family together, as you are praying like Jesus and through Jesus – asking, seeking, knocking, and speaking in persistent faith? How would the Lord have you make prayer a greater emphasis in your church life?

The first three cautions of carefulness for local church life that we have considered are to carefully ensure that we are believing, proclaiming, and living the truth of Jesus; prioritizing and demonstrating the love of Jesus; and that with persistent faith, we are praying like Jesus.

4. Being Careful to Seek Unity Like Jesus: making
every effort. This is made possible for us by God
the Holy Spirit, who is the Spirit of unity.

The apostle Paul used strong language on this theme when exhorting the church of Ephesus to do this. Writing from the isolation of a prison cell, and with palpable concern and love for the church of Ephesus, Paul wrote:

> *I, a prisoner for serving the Lord, beg you to lead a life worthy of your calling, for you have been called by God. Always be humble and gentle. Be patient with each other, making allowance for each other's faults because of your love. Make every effort to keep yourselves united in the Spirit, binding yourselves together with peace.* (Ephesians 4:1-3)

Paul was pleading with the leaders and members of the church in Ephesus to *make every effort to keep [themselves] united in the Spirit.* We must all agree with Paul's assessment that unity in the church does not and will not automatically or easily happen. It requires our effort. Even when a local church is experiencing a good degree of unity with one another, it will require effort to retain that unity.

Unity in the Holy Spirit must always be maintained by our love, listening, prayerfulness, and, as we have seen, by having a shared desire to please and honor Jesus Christ, whom we all confess to be the head of His Body, the Church. Paul begs the Ephesian church to make this their goal and practice, for this is part of living a life that is worthy of our calling.

Paul instructed the church about what is needed for biblical church unity to be attained. Unity in the Holy Spirit happens when, with God's help, we are making a prayerful effort to *always be humble and gentle* with one another. Unity in the church requires us to be *patient with each other* and *make allowance for each other's faults*, even as we also lovingly teach, rebuke, correct, and train (2 Timothy 3:16).

What is it that motivates the church to such humility, gentleness, patience, and allowance for one another's faults? It is *because of [our] love*. This is our clear biblical guidance on what it means to *make every effort to keep yourselves united in the Spirit, binding yourselves together with peace.*

Notice that we are told to make every effort to retain the unity that binds people together in God's peace. We are not told to create such unity, for we cannot, and we do not need to do so, for this has already been done for us by Jesus Christ and through the Holy Spirit. Rather, the church is to guard the unity, or *make every effort* to keep it.

So local church leaders are given this caution of carefulness for biblical church governance. We cannot allow the church to be governed in disunity, because when that happens, it is clear that Jesus Christ is not being allowed His rightful place as head of the Church. And when disunity and division are allowed to fester, biblical principles are being ignored, and the Holy Spirit is not being sought together.

Even if and when the local church experiences a good degree of unity with one another, as the Bible exhorts us, we are to carefully ensure that we *make every effort* to keep it. How does this happen? It will happen through humble prayer and by seeking and allowing the character of Jesus to dwell in us and among us by faith.

Applications: What are some applications for ensuring in our local church life that we are seeking to unite like Jesus, making every effort to maintain the unity that is made possible for us by God the Holy Spirit, who is the Spirit of unity?

1. We can train, disciple, encourage, and help one another to be prayerfully seeking unity in the Holy Spirit by desiring and seeking only what Jesus wants, and by demonstrating the character of Jesus with one another through humility, gentleness, and merciful allowance for one another's faults, always being motivated by His love.

2. In our preaching, teaching, discipling, and conversing with one another within the church family, we can make every effort for biblical unity by bathing our decisions in prayer and every action in love by laying aside personal agendas and replacing them with love for God and one another.

3. Church leaders can live and lead in biblical unity with one another as Jesus prayed, guiding the church to seek the mind of Christ in the unity of the Holy Spirit.

For personal reflection: What are some implications for you personally of God's call for you to make every effort for unity in Christ through the Holy Spirit?

For local church leaders' discussion: What are some implications for you as church leaders, and for your congregation collectively, that you have been called by God to make every effort to be united in and for Jesus Christ, and to do so in and by the Holy Spirit of unity? How can you apply this in your leadership meetings and decisions, and in your church meetings and decisions?

An Addendum

Practicing Biblical Congregationalism

Throughout history, Christians who are equally committed to the Lord Jesus Christ and to the truth and authority of the Bible have come to differing conclusions on various secondary matters of faith and practice. Church polity is one of those areas.

Christ's Church is not exclusive to one form of church structure and polity. The biblical principles we have considered are applicable for all local churches that love Jesus Christ and believe in Him, and that long to faithfully follow Him.

I have been greatly enriched throughout my lifetime of serving Jesus with friendships and fellowship with Christian brothers and sisters from many different denominations, theological persuasions, and structures of church governance. In my undergraduate years, I attended Barrington College in Rhode Island, where I majored in biblical studies. Barrington was a Christian liberal arts college with students from a variety of church backgrounds and theological perspectives.

Through those friendships and heart-to-heart discussions about the Bible and various matters of biblical theology and practice, my Lord taught me that Christians equally committed to the Lord and to His Word may disagree on many things, as long as we agree on main things. I learned that the main things include the saving gospel of Jesus Christ, who is the incarnate Son of God who died on the cross for our salvation, and that faith in Him is the only way of salvation. I also learned that it is indeed a main thing to believe that the Bible is God's inspired and infallible truth.

But my fellowship with diverse brothers and sisters in Jesus Christ also taught me that Christians who are fully agreed on the main things, including that the Bible is true and is our ultimate authority in our faith and practice, can have quite different understandings on many other things and still be one family of God together. Included among our differences is the structure of our biblical church polity.

But in this addendum, my focus is on biblical congregational governance because my own understanding, calling, and ministry experience have been within this framework. Congregationalism is what I was called to live. I was raised in Baptist churches that practiced congregational governance under Christ's headship. I have attended two seminaries, both of which affirmed congregational polity, and in God's leading I have served three local churches, each of which aimed to be congregational.

For more than four decades, I served in a denomination that I loved and that was comprised of congregational ministers and churches. For eight of those years, I served in a national leadership role of that faith group as Conference Minister of the Conservative Congregational Christian Conference (CCCC).

This addendum is addressed to Christians and local churches that long to follow Jesus biblically and congregationally. I'll touch briefly on Congregationalism in history. I'll also share some history being made now through the international connections of the World Evangelical Congregational Fellowship (WECF), and in the faith, polity, and covenant still shared among biblical Congregationalists.

Biblical Congregationalism in Church History

In Early Church History

The form of biblical church polity now called congregationalism was evident early in church history. When certain disciples of Jesus Christ in a local church were recognized by members of that church as having the requisite spiritual gifts and anointing of God for a particular work, it was the congregation together that set them apart for that work.

In the inspired book of Acts, which describes for us the birth and earliest days of the Church, several occasions of this are seen. Christians in a particular local congregation prayerfully discerned the mind of Christ and then proceeded in unity together. Examples include:

When choosing deacons: *"Therefore, brothers, pick out from among you seven men of good repute, full of the Spirit and of wisdom, whom we will appoint to this duty. But we will devote ourselves to prayer and to the ministry of the word." And what they said pleased the whole gathering, and they chose Stephen, a man full of faith and of the Holy Spirit, and Philip, and Prochorus, and Nicanor, and Timon, and Parmenas, and Nicolaus, a proselyte of Antioch* (Acts 6:3-5 ESV).

When choosing missionaries: *Now there were in the church at Antioch prophets and teachers, Barnabas, Simeon who was called Niger, Lucius of Cyrene, Manaen a lifelong friend of Herod the tetrarch, and Saul. While they were worshiping the Lord and fasting, the Holy Spirit said, "Set apart for me Barnabas and Saul for the work to which I have called them." Then after fasting and praying they laid their hands on them and sent them off* (Acts 13:1-3 ESV).

When choosing more missionaries for a particular assignment: *Then it seemed good to the apostles and the elders, with the whole church, to choose men from among them and send them to Antioch with Paul and Barnabas. They sent Judas called Barsabbas, and Silas, leading men among the brothers, with the . . . letter. . . . So when they were sent off, they went down to Antioch, and having gathered the congregation together, they delivered the letter. And when they had read it, they rejoiced because of its encouragement. And Judas and Silas, who were themselves prophets, encouraged and strengthened the brothers with many words. And after they had spent some time, they were sent off in peace by the brothers to those who had sent them* (Acts 15:22-23, 30-33 ESV).

Later, when a local church was straying from truth, it was not only the individual leaders or plurality of designated leaders who were held responsible before God, but the entire local church was also responsible and accountable. Members were expected to address this together, as seen in Paul's letter to the churches in Galatia:

> *This letter is from Paul, an apostle. I was not appointed by any group of people or any human authority, but by Jesus Christ himself and by God the Father, who raised Jesus from*

*the dead. All the brothers and sisters here join me in sending
this letter to the churches of Galatia. May God the Father
and our Lord Jesus Christ give you grace and peace. Jesus
gave his life for our sins, just as God our Father planned, in
order to rescue us from this evil world in which we live. All
glory to God forever and ever! Amen.*

*I am shocked that you are turning away so soon from God,
who called you to himself through the loving mercy of Christ.
You are following a different way that pretends to be the
Good News.* (Galatians 1:1-6)

This was also seen in John's letters to churches of Asia Minor, as included
in Revelation 1-3. For example:
   This letter is from John to the seven churches in the province of Asia.

*Grace and peace to you from the one who is, who always
was, and who is still to come; from the sevenfold Spirit before
his throne; and from Jesus Christ. He is the faithful witness
to these things, the first to rise from the dead, and the ruler
of all the kings of the world.*

*All glory to him who loves us and has freed us from our sins
by shedding his blood for us. He has made us a Kingdom of
priests for God his Father. All glory and power to him forever
and ever! Amen.* (Revelation 1:4-6)

This is also seen in 1 Corinthians, which was addressed to the whole
church – that is, to all members:

*This letter is from Paul, chosen by the will of God to be an
apostle of Christ Jesus, and from our brother Sosthenes. I
am writing to God's church in Corinth, to you who have
been called by God to be his own holy people. He made you
holy by means of Christ Jesus, just as he did for all people
everywhere who call on the name of our Lord Jesus Christ,*

> *their Lord and ours. May God our Father and the Lord Jesus*
> *Christ give you grace and peace.* (1 Corinthians 1:1-3)

When addressing church discipline, Paul instructed the entire local church to do this together. For example, when confronting sexual immorality, which defiles the whole church, members were urged to address it collectively: *When you are assembled in the name of the Lord Jesus and my spirit is present, with the power of our Lord Jesus, you are to deliver this man to Satan for the destruction of the flesh, so that his spirit may be saved in the day of the Lord* (1 Corinthians 5:4-5 ESV).

From the very earliest days of the Christian Church, local churches have functioned as local congregations of Christ followers under the headship of Jesus. Local churches have understood that we share with one another the holy responsibility of being Christ's church in this generation and in this location.

For personal reflection: As you reflect on the earliest churches, how do you think they approached their decision-making and ministry congregationally under the headship of Jesus Christ, and what are some lessons for you from their example?

For local church leaders' discussion: What are some implications for you as leaders, and for your church family together, of the early Church's understanding, awareness of responsibility, and practice of congregational governance under Christ's headship?

In Reformation/Restoration History
Due to limited space, I cannot provide a detailed history of how the Holy Spirit inspired congregationalism or outline the histories of Baptist churches and others that adhere to congregational principles. Nor can I fully explore here how congregationalism has developed in all the nations where it currently thrives.

Most scholars agree that most of these movements, at least in part, derived from Spirit-led renewal initiatives in the seventeenth-century Church of England, which aimed to restore the Church's preaching, teaching, and practices according to the Bible. Two divergent tracks flowed into congregationalism, both of which longed for local churches to honor Jesus biblically.

Some sought separation from the Church of England in order to be independent and autonomous local churches under Christ's headship. These Christians were called Separatists. Others desired to remain in the Church of England in order to purify it by bringing the Church back to biblical principles and practices. These Christians were called Puritans.

The first person known to have specifically set out what came to be known as congregational principles was Robert Browne (1550–1633). He is sometimes referred to as the founder of Congregationalism. While studying for ordination in the Church of England, he felt called by God to come apart from that Church to form what was then referred to as a Separatist congregation. This was illegal and dangerous because it was considered treasonous against the king and his church.

In 1581, Browne and his followers moved to Holland to worship freely there. While in Holland, Browne wrote a number of essays laying out what he considered to be essential features of biblical Congregationalism. Primary among Browne's emphases was a conviction that biblical churches were to be comprised only of those who were regenerate and spiritually alive believers in Jesus Christ. He criticized the Anglican Church for including all citizens within the church. Browne also asserted that although every local church is independent before the Lord, they are still called to come together with other churches for shared ministry and concerns.

John Cotton (1585-1652) was an English clergyman whose stated aim was to restore the Church of England back to biblical practices. He was not a Separatist, in that he did not want to separate from the organized Church. Cotton was a Nonconformist who longed for the Church to be purified. He was thus called a Puritan.

When John Cotton eventually lost all freedom to worship according to his biblical convictions, he emigrated to the American colonies, having received a written invitation from church leaders in the Massachusetts Bay Colony to join them in New England. Cotton became the preeminent minister and theologian of the Massachusetts Bay Colony.

A great part of his efforts during his later ministry was devoted to the governance of New England churches that were congregational. Cotton is the one who gave the name "Congregationalism" to this form of church polity. He was a key leader of the Cambridge Synod, which convened off and on from 1646-1648 in Cambridge, Massachusetts, with church leaders from throughout the Puritan colonies.

Out of this synod came the "Cambridge Platform," which was the foundational document of New England Congregationalism. It outlined the biblical principles of congregational governance, emphasizing the autonomy of every local church under the headship of Jesus Christ.

The synod adopted the doctrinal statement of the Westminster Confession of Faith, which had been written by English Puritans. Although the Cambridge Synod disagreed with the portions of the Westminster Confession regarding presbyterian polity, they affirmed this doctrinal statement for congregational churches, stating that they "do judge it to be very holy, orthodox, and judicious in all matters of faith; and do therefore freely and fully consent thereunto, for the substance thereof."[26]

Ten years after the Cambridge Platform was published in New England, English Congregationalists convened a conference of church leaders at Savoy Palace in London. From that convention came the Savoy Declaration. Its full title was "A Declaration of the Faith and Order Owned and Practiced in the Congregational Churches in England."

Greg Strand is the Evangelical Free Church of America's executive director of theology and credentialing. The EFCA is a denomination of ministers and churches that also aims to practice congregational governance. Speaking about the 1658 Savoy Declaration, Strand wrote that it "affirmed Congregationalists' unity with the broader Christian and Reformed faith, addressed misconceptions about the Free churches, and outlined their differences with the established church in matters of church governance."[27] Strand rightly observed that the Savoy Declaration still provides a beautiful standard for congregationalist churches.

Alwyn York, who has served for many years as historian of the Conservative Congregational Christian Conference, commends both the Cambridge Platform and the Savoy Confession of Faith for contemporary Congregationalists. He recommends that all ministers and churches who aim to be congregational in governance and biblical in theology

---

26 Albert E. Dunning, *Congregationalists in America: A Popular History of Their Origin, Belief, Polity, Growth, and Work* (New York: J. A. Hill & Co., 1894), 148.

27 Greg Strand, "Beautiful Standard, Healthy Model: The Savoy Declaration," The Gospel Coalition, November 25, 2022, https://www.thegospelcoalition.org/article/savoy-declaration/.

should study these foundational documents, because the principles they contain are timeless.[28] These documents are included in the book *Historic Documents of Congregationalism*, edited by Robert E. Davis.

For personal reflection: What applications do you see from the example of early Separatists and Puritans who so deeply longed for the Church to be brought back to biblical principles of governance under the headship of Jesus?

For local church leaders' discussion: What are implications or applications for you as leaders, and for your congregation, of the deeply held motivations of your spiritual ancestors to worship freely no matter the cost, according to biblical convictions?

In World Missions:
Missionary Outreach of Biblical Congregationalists
The early Church was exceptionally missional because the Great Commission was so clear and fresh, and the good news of Jesus was too wonderful to be kept quiet. The Church took seriously the Lord's command: *Go and make disciples of all the nations, baptizing them in the name of the Father and the Son and the Holy Spirit. Teach these new disciples to obey all the commands I have given you. And be sure of this: I am with you always, even to the end of the age* (Matthew 28:19-20).

The local *ekklesia* in Antioch surely had a vision to take the good news of Jesus Christ to places and people who had not yet heard the way of salvation. Therefore, they prayerfully commissioned and sent out Barnabas and Saul (Acts 13:2-3). The good news of Jesus Christ was spread, people came to faith in Him, and new churches were established. As the churches focused on spreading the good news of the gospel, the Church expanded throughout the Roman Empire and beyond.

By AD 300, according to some estimates, about 10 percent of the Roman population followed Jesus Christ, and by God's amazing grace, by AD 350, Christianity had reached more than 50 percent of the Roman Empire. This growth was a direct result of local churches responding to the Lord's call to send and to go as missionaries with the good news.[29]

---

28 Alwyn York, *Rediscovering Congregational Foundations* (Minneapolis: Foresee Publications, 2010), 21-31

29 Rodney Stark, *The Rise of Christianity: A Sociologist Reconsiders History* (Princeton: Princeton University Press, 1996), 19.

Biblical Congregationalism has long had this vision because Jesus Christ calls us to it. Local congregations that are following Jesus will look beyond themselves to prayerfully discern those to whom God is sending them. The first mission-sending agency established in the United States was begun by the congregational churches.

Philip Corr tells this story in his well-researched chapter on "A History of Congregational Missions." He begins: "In 1806 a small group of Williams College students met to discuss the spiritual condition of the Asian nations. A storm arose and they took shelter in a haystack. From this 'Haystack Prayer Meeting' came the resolve to take the gospel to those who had not heard it."[30] When those young students brought their biblical plea to leaders of their congregational churches, the Lord began directing the churches to respond with a shared vision. In 1812, the first missionary-sending agency, the American Board of Commissioners for Foreign Missions, was established.

In *There Are Modern Day Pilgrims*, Rod Wetzig told of even earlier missionary efforts by English Congregationalists. Through the London Missionary Society, missionaries were sent out to proclaim the gospel and plant churches in places where the gospel was not yet known.[31]

The London Missionary Society was an interdenominational evangelical missionary society formed in England in 1795. It was started at the urging of Welsh Congregationalist minister Edward Williams. The shared vision among participating churches was to fulfill the Great Commission given by Jesus to bring His saving gospel to the world.

There are many wonderful examples of lasting fruitfulness from the faithful outreach of early Congregational missions. One example is given by Rod Wetzig and Bob Wilber, whose work in Micronesia was influenced by results of that outreach. They describe how in 1819, Congregational missionaries were commissioned and sent out from the Park Street Church in Boston, Massachusetts, to bring the gospel of Jesus Christ to the Sandwich Islands, which are now called the Hawaiian Islands.[32]

---

30   Philip Corr, "A History of Congregational Missions," in *Modern Day Pilgrims—A Proud Heritage* (The History of the Conservative Congregational Conference), (Lake Elmo, MN: Foresee Publications, 2023), 190.

31   Rod Wetzig, *There Are Modern Day Pilgrims* (Lake Elmo, MN: Foresee Publications, 2011), 65.

32   Rod Wetzig and Bob Wilber, "Ministry in Micronesia," in *Modern Day Pilgrims*, 241-245.

By 1850, the Hawaiian church was very well established. In 1851, more Congregational missionaries were commissioned and sent out from Boston. They headed to islands even further west of the Hawaiian Islands, known as the Marshall Islands and Micronesia. On their way westward, those missionaries stopped in Hawaii, where a group of Hawaiian Christians joined them. Together they evangelized and planted new churches, and for the next one hundred years, Congregational missionaries worked to strengthen those churches.

Another beautiful example of Congregational missionary work was told by Hristo Kulichev, a Bulgarian pastor whom I was blessed to meet many years ago, and whose personal story of suffering for the gospel of Jesus was very inspiring to me and to many others. In his book *Heralds of the Truth*, Hristo described his imprisonment for preaching the good news of Jesus. He told of hardships that were experienced by those who came to Bulgaria with the message of salvation by grace and through faith in Jesus Christ.

Many years ago when I visited Bulgaria, I stood outside the meetinghouse of the Congregational church in Plovdiv, where I observed an old monument to the missionary couple who first brought the gospel of Jesus Christ to that city and region, and who gave their lives in doing so. Their names were William and Susan Meriam. Their story is told by Hristo Kulichev in his book. These and other Congregational missionaries were commissioned and sent to Bulgaria by the American Board of Commissioners for Foreign Missions (ABCFM).[33]

Kulichev summarized the dedication of the missionaries, saying, "The missionaries were people of strong faith, devoted to God, kind-spirited, and highly educated. Some had doctoral degrees and almost all of them were ordained pastors. Having left their countries and their serenity, risking their lives, they arrived in the under-developed Turkish Empire. They waded into the mud of the Orient, the village dogs barking at them, people flinging stones and heaping abuse on them."[34]

For personal reflection: To what degree have you shared the missionary heart of early Congregationalists? Will you now ask the Lord for such a vision?

---

33   Hristo Kulichev, *Heralds of the Truth: The History of the Evangelical Church in Bulgaria.* Originally published by the Bulgarian Bible Society. English version published by Lulu. com (2010), 32-35.

34   Kulichev, *Heralds of the Truth*, 48.

For local church leaders' discussion: How does your local church currently reflect the missionary heart of early Congregationalists, or how could you possibly strengthen the missionary vision within your congregation?

Making Congregational History Now

The World Evangelical Congregational Fellowship (WECF)

In the 1980s, God began connecting various international fellowships of biblical Congregational churches. Clifford Christensen, who served as Conference Minister of the Conservative Congregational Christian Conference (USA) from 1981-2003, described how the World Evangelical Congregational Fellowship (WECF) came to be. In 1983 at the annual gathering of the CCCC (USA), the Lord connected leaders of evangelical Congregational fellowships from the USA, Australia, Great Britain, and Micronesia. These representatives had a common vision.[35]

They agreed that "the ties between Evangelical Congregationalists from around the world needed to be strengthened, and there needed to be a means by which effective communication and joint ministries could be carried out. The formation of an international evangelical Congregational union was proposed, and it was agreed to meet together in a year for further discussion."[36]

In 1984, a second meeting was held with representatives of the above-listed nations, plus a representative from Brazil, at which time it was decided to "form an international fellowship to be called the World Evangelical Congregational Fellowship (WECF), and the first three articles of its constitution were written."[37]

It was later decided that the inaugural assembly of the WECF would be held in England on October 15-18, 1986. Clifford Christensen, who served as the first president of this international fellowship, described its origin in this way:

---

35   Clifford Christensen, *Modern Day Pilgrims: A Proud Heritage* (Lake Elmo, MN: Conservative Congregational Christian Conference, 2023), 247-259.

36   Christensen, *Modern Day Pilgrims*, 247.

37   Christensen, *Modern Day Pilgrims*, 248.

Throughout the process of forming the WECF there was a wonderful sense of God's providence. When the idea of such a fellowship surfaced in 1983, it seemed to come to several hearts at once. There had been an earlier attempt in 1966 to form an international Evangelical Congregational Union. A constitution had even been drawn up, . . . but the timing was not right. The EFCC and the FCC as well as several other founding members of the WECF did not exist. Twenty years later the timing was right and the WECF was born. The feeling of those present at the inaugural assembly in London was that this was a "gathering" rather than a planned event. God has "gathered" us together into a new fellowship of evangelical Congregationalists from around the world.[38]

The first meeting included representatives of these fellowships who had previously voted to join the WECF. These representatives were:

- The Fellowship of Congregational Churches of Australia

- The Congregational Union of Ireland

- The Union of Congregational Churches of Portugal

- The Conservative Congregational Christian Conference of United States

There were some other groups that voted to join but were not represented at the first meeting. These groups included:

- The United Churches of Christ of Moen, Truk, in Micronesia

- The Congregational Union of New Zealand

- The Evangelical Fellowship of Congregational Churches of South Africa

Since the WECF's formal inception in 1986, the Lord has drawn more fellowships of evangelical Congregational churches into the WECF family, including the following:

---

38   Christensen, *Modern Day Pilgrims*, 248.

- The Evangelical Congregational Churches of Argentina

- The Alliance of Evangelical Congregational Churches, Brazil

- The Union of Evangelical Congregational Churches, Brazil

- The Union of Congregational Churches in Bulgaria

- The Congregational Christian Churches in Canada

- Evangelical Churches Association (Congregational) Manipur, India

- Evangesko-Kongresanka Crkva Skopje, Republic of North Macedonia

- Chuuk Congregational Church of Christ, Federated States of Micronesia

- Evangelical Church of Myanmar

- Evangelical Congregational Churches of Nepal

- National Association of Congregational Churches, Philippines

- Congregational Church of Jesus in Samoa

The threefold purpose of the WECF is stated in Article 3 of its constitution:

1. To promote fellowship and cooperative endeavour in the faith, polity and work of evangelical Congregational associations and churches throughout the world.

2. To preserve the historic Congregational commitment to the Lordship of Christ and the infallibility of His Word, and

3. To present to the world a witness to our oneness in Christ as evangelical Congregationalists.[39]

I have been enormously blessed to visit with brothers and sisters in Christ in ten member fellowships of the World Evangelical Congregational Fellowship, and in every case, I have rejoiced to see and to share a common commitment to be the Church of Jesus Christ according to the guidance of Scripture. I

---

39   https://cong-wecf.org/constitution/.

have been encouraged by the evident and mutual passion to be local churches that love Jesus and one another, and to be disciples who make disciples.

Biblical Congregationalists in any culture or nation will understand that the Lord of their lives and the head of their local churches is Jesus Christ. They therefore feel kinship with others who share such sacred conviction and commitment. The WECF is a beautiful illustration of this, as members interface with one another, learn from one another, pray for one another, and work together to advance the kingdom of Jesus Christ.

For personal reflection: What does it mean to you and how have you benefited from being part of the worldwide Church?

For local church leaders' discussion: How is your local church currently experiencing connections with the worldwide church, or what could you do to strengthen such connections?

What Do Biblical Congregationalists Still Share? Faith, Polity, Covenants

The Faith of Biblical Congregationalists Today

The WECF constitution outlines our common faith as biblical Congregationalists in this way:

While we acknowledge the Savoy Declaration of Faith and Order to be the classical expression of historic Congregationalism and, therefore, a valuable guideline for Congregational churches, we affirm the following statement of faith as an adequate basis for fellowship among evangelical Congregationalists.

1. We believe the Bible, consisting of the Old and New Testaments, to be the only inspired, inerrant, infallible, authoritative Word of God written.

2. We believe that there is one God, eternally existent in three persons: Father, Son and Holy Ghost.

3. We believe in the deity of Christ, in His virgin birth, and His

sinless life, in His miracles, in His vicarious and atoning death through His shed blood, in His bodily resurrection, in His ascension to the right hand of the Father, and in His personal return in power and glory.

4. We believe that the salvation of lost and sinful man is through justification by faith apart from works and that regeneration by the Holy Spirit is absolutely essential.

5. We believe in the present ministry of the Holy Spirit by whose indwelling power and fullness the Christian is enabled to live a godly life in this present evil world.

6. We believe in the resurrection of both the saved and the lost; they that are saved unto the resurrection of life, and they that are lost unto the resurrection of damnation.

7. We believe in the spiritual unity of all believers in Christ.

Members of the WECF affirm that as biblical Congregational Christians we agree on the truth of these seven statements. Beyond these core statements, however, we acknowledge and appreciate that Christians and local churches of sincere faith in the Lord Jesus Christ and in the supreme authority of the Bible may understand differently other secondary matters of faith.

We further believe that our Lord does not want us to divide over such differences, but rather, Paul tells us to *make every effort to keep yourselves united in the Spirit, . . . just as you have been called to one glorious hope for the future* (Ephesians 4:3-4). We believe that this divine injunction applies to all of our local churches, to our various national fellowships of evangelical ministers and Congregational churches, and also to our international fellowship.

For personal reflection: What does it mean to you to share faith convictions with Christians throughout history, and with Christians now throughout the world?

For local church leaders' discussion: How well do your church members understand the fundamentals of biblical faith, both historically and globally? What actions can you take to enhance their appreciation?

The Polity of Biblical Congregationalists Today

The WECF constitution outlines our common polity among biblical Congregationalists in this way:

1. We believe that Jesus Christ is the head of His Body, the Church universal, and of each local church.

2. We believe that each local church is in itself a complete church, and therefore autonomous and possesses all rights and responsibilities of the Church by the Holy Spirit as set forth in the Holy Scriptures.

3. We believe that Jesus Christ exercises His authority in each local church by the Holy Spirit through the Holy Scriptures.

4. We believe that each local church is ultimately answerable only to Jesus Christ, and not to any association, conference, council, synod or any other ecclesiastical body.

5. We believe that it is proper and beneficial for each local church to seek fellowship and counsel of other such local churches.

The WECF affirms that as biblical Congregational Christians, we fully agree on the truth of these five statements regarding local church governance. Beyond these core statements, however, we understand that Christians and local churches of sincere faith in Jesus and in the authority of the Bible may choose to be structured differently, and again we know that Jesus would not have us divide over such differences.

Congregationalists must recognize that a particular risk in our form of polity is wrongly presuming that this church belongs to us, so therefore the decisions are ours to make. Church leaders and local churches can too easily fall prey to this perspective. Rather, biblical Congregational governance is to be a continual reminder of our dependence:

- Upon Jesus Christ, who is head of His entire church, and of every local church.

- Upon the Bible as our ultimate standard in faith and practice. This conviction requires studying and searching the Scriptures as our way of life, seeking and hearing the Lord's Word, and discerning and doing His will in every decision.

- Upon the Holy Spirit for anointing and power in ministry, for revelation of truth, for clear guidance, and for unity in our diversity.

- Upon prayer – that as individuals, families, church leaders, and local churches we will truly devote ourselves to prayer (Acts 2:42; Colossians 4:12), believing that God can and surely will make a way where there seems to be no way.

For personal reflection: What could be some implications for you personally of affirming the above listed principles of Biblical congregational polity?

For local church leaders' discussion: Review again the five statements of congregational polity listed above from the WECF constitution. What are some implications of each of these statements for you as church leaders, and for your local congregation together?

The Covenants of Biblical Congregationalists Today
The biblical concept of covenant has been emphasized in historic Congregationalism. Foundational documents of Congregationalism, such as the Cambridge Platform, outlined necessary covenant commitments in local church communities.[40] A church covenant is essentially a shared declaration that local churches call their members to sign, thus affirming their agreed upon responsibilities as church members to God and to one another. Covenants were and are intended to strengthen the community by solidifying commitment.

Early Congregationalists in New England colonies developed a system in which every local community organized a gathered church (*ekklesia*) of believers in Jesus. Church members were those who were thought to be among the elect and could therefore give an account of their conversion.

---

40   See for example, Robert E. Davis, *Historic Documents of Congregationalism* (Miller Falls, MA: Puritan Press, 2005), 95-97.

James F. Cooper described this practice in this way: "Likewise, though it had been practiced in New England for several years, they reaffirmed from First Corinthians that 'churches should be churches of saints' and must therefore require of its members a test of grace, or conversion."[41]

Every local church was thus founded upon a church covenant, which was a written agreement signed by all members in which they agreed to uphold certain congregational principles, to be guided by the Scriptures alone (sola scriptura) in their decision-making, and to submit to church discipline. The right and responsibility of each congregation to elect its own officers and manage its own affairs was upheld.

Local Congregational churches in early New England were formed in this manner: "There the saints formed churches from nothing. A meeting of the community identified a small group... to serve as the pillars of their church. These men drafted a formal covenant in which they pledged to join in the proper worship of God and to nourish each other in the search for further religious truth. They then extended invitations to others in the community to join them by swearing to the covenant, admitting as members those who had an understanding of the faith and also a reputation for godliness.".[42] Affirming a shared covenant of faith and commitment to follow Jesus Christ together was and is a key aspect of practicing biblical Congregationalism.

During my lifetime, I have affirmed just two formal covenants. At twenty-one years of age, before God, family, and friends, I entered into a marriage covenant with my dear wife, Helen. This was for me a solemn yet very joyful covenant "until death separates us."

The second type of formal covenant I have affirmed before God, my family, and friends is a local-church membership covenant. Several times as a member of a local church, and three times as a called pastor of a particular local church, I have covenanted with the congregation, affirming our shared faith and my commitment to live among them and before God in a certain way.

Though local-church covenants originated in English Puritanism, in time they became common in many congregationally governed Baptist churches, and in similar "free church" and nondenominational

---

41   James F. Cooper Jr., *Tenacious of Their Liberties: The Congregationalists in Colonial Massachusetts* (New York: Oxford University Press, 1999), 17, 19.

42   Francis J. Bremer, *Puritanism: A Very Short Introduction* (New York: Oxford University Press, 2009), 69-70

fellowships that aim to apply biblical principles of Congregationalism in their local church governance.

Some local church covenants I have seen are many generations old, for the truth of God has not changed, nor has the call to obedience in following Jesus. I have known churches that invite their members every year to reaffirm and sign again the church covenant they have made to each other and to God. This serves well to remind members of their commitment to one another as they renew their vows before God.

Other local churches design their local church covenant on biblical principles, but use fresh language – as, for example, Pastor P. J. Tibayan, pastor of the Bellflower Baptist Church near Los Angeles, who is also the leader of the Gospel Coalition in Los Angeles County. In writing a sample church covenant, he was clearly inspired by the "one another" commands of the New Testament:

> We renew afresh our covenant together before our Lord Jesus Christ to be members of one another, honor one another, live in harmony with one another, maintain unity with one another, build one another up, be like-minded towards one another, accept one another, care for one another, serve one another, bear one another's burdens, be kind to one another, forgive one another, abound in love towards one another, comfort one another, encourage one another, stir one another up to love and good works not neglecting to meet together, confess our sins to one another, pray for one another, admonish one another, hold one another accountable as a church, be hospitable to one another, greet one another, fellowship with one another, listen to one another, speak the truth to one another, submit to one another while not passing judgment on one another, not provoking one another, not envying one another, not hating one another, not slandering one another, and not bearing grudges against one another as we strive side by side with one another for the faith of the gospel.

> We do all this because Christ has loved and continues to love us in each of these ways and this frees our hearts to

love one another as he has loved us. May the grace of the
Lord Jesus Christ, the love of God, and the fellowship of
the Holy Spirit be with us all. Amen.[43]

Though all biblical and congregationally governed churches may not include a formal covenant as part of their commitments to one another before Jesus Christ, all affirm agreement concerning foundational biblical principles and doctrines, and all confirm before the Lord and one another that they have decided to follow Jesus, and desire to do so together.

As a part of affirming our shared biblical commitments, and to reaffirm together our promises to walk with one another along this journey, it could be helpful to learn a lesson from Christians who preceded us as local churches of Christ followers. It might be helpful to consider drafting and affirming a biblical covenant for your local congregation.

Imagine being part of a local church in which members are discipled to truly know that Jesus calls us to a serious covenant relationship with Him and with each other. Imagine being a congregation that covenants to live like this! Local church covenants of biblical Congregationalism can help to remind us of the faithfulness of God and of the promises we have made to God and to each other as we follow Jesus together.

For personal reflection: What covenants have you ever made before God and others? When and why, and what was the result? What sort of covenant would you be willing to make with God and the members of your local church, and why?

For local church leaders' discussion: What covenants have you made with each other before God as leaders and friends? Has your local church made any covenants with one another before God? If so, how, when, and why? If not, why not?

---

43   P. J. Tibayan, "Six Sample Church Covenants," February 19, 2015, https://pjtibayan.word-press.com/2015/02/19/six-sample-church-covenants/.

Other Titles by
Stephen A. Gammon

Because God . . . I Can
by Stephen Gammon

Because God is personal and relational, He desires a personal relationship with every one of us. God invites us to come apart each day for some quiet time with Jesus. When we do this, our Lord speaks and we hear; then He hears as we share our hearts, and He changes us in His presence.

Daily quiet times with Jesus are an amazing and treasured opportunity. The life-changing principle we can apply in His presence each day is *Because God . . . I Can*. Because God what? Because He speaks, acts, reveals, empowers, loves – because He is with me in this moment and always, I can.

What can I be or do because of who God is and what He does? This devotional focuses on twelve foundational practices we are called and enabled to live as we walk with God. Each month a different practice is emphasized that I can live today *Because God . . .* Each day of the month another truth about God is highlighted regarding that theme, which leads to increasingly understand how *I Can* be living this practice today.

Available where books are sold.

Walking with God through Deep Valleys
by Stephen Gammon

All of life is not lived on mountaintops. We will experience some deep valleys of pain, disappointment, uncertainty, sickness, grief, and even *the valley of the shadow of death*. Sometimes multitudes enter long and deep valleys together, as in prolonged seasons of war, or the COVID-19 pandemic that brought many to hardship, uncertainty, and fear. Yet, it often feels like we are walking through a deep valley alone. It doesn't have to be that way – Scripture makes it clear that if we have even a little faith, the Lord walks with us and guides us. If we keep our eyes on Him, our deepest valleys will strengthen and enrich our walk with God.

Stephen Gammon faithfully served God for 40 years as a pastor and military chaplain. Then, in October 2018, he was diagnosed with cancer (Multiple Myeloma); he and his wife Helen entered this deep valley, walking with God by faith. With personal vulnerability and spiritual insight, he posted regular medical updates on the CaringBridge website, sharing many priceless lessons learned while walking with God through their valley. Tens of thousands of online visits and innumerable personal responses and reflections from readers attest to the power of these truths. Now edited and published in this book, these lessons will point you towards genuine contentment and peace as you walk through your own deep valleys.

Available where books are sold.

Walking With God
by Stephen Gammon

Are you longing to walk closer to God, or wondering if it's even really possible? Would you and your sphere of influence benefit from being mentored for a lifetime of walking with God? Or, are you a minister leading people of various ages and in various seasons of life, but finding it difficult to relate to them?

God teaches priceless lessons through life, including some we may resist learning. Dr. Stephen Gammon shares timeless biblical wisdom and treasured personal insights learned through 14 successive chapters of life in Walking With God: 101 Lessons for Life and Ministry. Applying these lessons will…

- Heighten your enjoyment of walking with God

- Expand your awareness of lessons God is trying to teach you

- Reduce your resistance to leaving your comfort zone in obedience to Jesus

- Increase your anticipation of fruitful ministry for Christ until your last breath

Available where books are sold.

www.ingramcontent.com/pod-product-compliance
Lightning Source LLC
Chambersburg PA
CBHW061745120626
46550CB00005B/1896